The Keys to the House, Tree, and Person

Paul Pitner

Diablo Valley College

KENDALL/HUNT PUBLISHING COMPANY
4050 Westmark Drive   Dubuque, Iowa 52002

Cover image courtesy of Corel.

Copyright © 2004 by Paul Pitner

ISBN 978-0-7575-1298-8

Printed in the United States of America
10 9 8 7 6 5 4 3

—For Julia and Gail

Contents

Acknowledgments

This book would not have been possible without the inspiration and perspiration of Kenneth Leighton. His tireless work, advising, and editing of the content cannot be repaid. At a time when others doubted, or when my own self doubts crept in, he championed me and buoyed my spirit. The fact that he believes that I have produced a worthwhile book is more than enough satisfaction for me.

I would also like to thank Glenda Fuge for providing valuable insight and information over many years of friendship.

A special thanks to Beth Bunnenberg for teaching me all I know about my craft and the art of looking at art.

Thanks to Rick Risbrough for mentoring me and providing me with a safe harbor for my teaching career.

Thank you to the students of Diablo Valley College who provided me their art.

Introduction

Drawing is an activity of childhood. The rate of art production steadily declines into adulthood, where little or none is produced. For the child, the process of producing artwork is more important than what the end product is—what it looks like. In other words, the process of making something is meaningful; it taps into psychological needs for self-expression. The great artist is not so concerned about how the product of his or her work is perceived as much as how meaningful and expressive the artwork is for that artist. When people view art, they appreciate what it looks like and how it makes them feel. The art is salient; it has meaning to the viewer. The viewer is able to relate and connect with the artist through the artwork at a human and psychological level. Every drawing in *The Keys to the House, Tree, and Person* was chosen because of its potential saliency to the reader.

The artist who produces a picture of a house, a tree, and a person generates a work that has significant meaning to that artist, although he or she may not be aware of it. This book, *The Keys to the House, Tree, and Person,* provides the opportunity to get at the meaning behind the drawing. This book provides an opening into the psychological process that created the artwork. Unfortunately, most people get cut off from the process of producing art. For this there are many reasons, some of which are explored in this text. Fortunately, one does not have to be able to draw well in order to produce a house, a tree, and a person that can be analyzed.

Drawing ability does not affect the depth or scope of the analysis. This drawing exercise is about the *process,* not the product. When a drawing is produced, the drawer is analyzed through the drawing. This text provides a unique opportunity for the reader. This text asks the reader to produce a drawing and then walks the reader through an in-depth self-analysis of that drawing. Never before has such an interactive text been produced in the field of psychology. The projective test, "House, Tree, Person," traditionally used by psychologists as a diagnostic test for children, has rarely been applied to adults, thus making this text unique. A major highlight of this work is the vivid illustrations of actual drawings from students and clinical patients that are woven throughout the text.

This book also provides readers with the opportunity to measure stress levels, find their learning style, assess their self-esteem, and get an indication whether they or anyone else they know might have Attention Deficit Disorder with or without Hyperactivity. This text also contains a concise explanation of Freudian theory.

Enjoy this process of self-discovery; it's a fascinating endeavor and one which can be quite revealing.

STOP!
Draw a Picture
That Includes:
A House
A Tree &
A Person.
Use detail.

Draw a picture that includes a House, a Tree, and a Person. Draw the picture any way you want. You may only be able to draw stick figures, which are acceptable. This activity is not about drawing abilities; rather, it is about psychological principles. Even if you can only draw stick figures, at least spend some time putting details in your drawing. The more time and detail you spend on the drawing, the more potential information you will get from your analysis of it.

chapter 1

Theory Behind the Interpretation

PROJECTIVE TESTS: A DEFINITION

A House, a Tree, and a Person drawing is what is known as a projective test—the artist is projecting something of himself or herself on the ambiguous stimuli of the (blank) paper, having been prompted by the words: house, tree, and person. As with a movie projector, the artist is projecting unconscious aspects of himself or herself onto the paper. Since two drawings are never the same, this is a unique production of the artist.

FREUDIAN THEORY AND PROJECTIVE TESTS

Sigmund Freud proposed that almost all our behavior is directed by our unconscious mind, and this includes our drawing behavior. This unconscious mind does not speak to us in a language of words, but rather one of images. Think about your experiences with your dreams. They are a series of images and emotions related to those images. Freud referred to dreams as the road to the unconscious (*The Interpretation of Dreams,* 1900). He also referred to dreams as wish fulfillment. Those things we experience and cannot have in our waking life we can dream about having. According to Freud, much of what we want is disturbing to us, so our minds disguise the wish in the language of the unconscious images, thus creating a dream. When we become versed in the language of the unconscious, we are able to analyze these images. Then we begin to understand our dreams and other reflections of our unconscious, such as our drawings. These drawings, like our dreams, are little wishes. Freud's theory is that there are no accidents in life and that everything we do is purposeful, which means what one puts in his or her drawing is just as significant as what he or she does not put in it. When we say: "I forgot," Freud would counter: "Exactly, you chose to forget."

JUNGIAN THEORY AND HOW IT APPLIES TO THE ANALYSIS OF THE DRAWING

You will specifically analyze your drawing by using the ideas of another theorist, Carl Jung. Jung expanded on Freud's ideas by proposing that there are two types of unconscious mind: a Personal Unconscious, which corresponds to Freud's idea of unconscious, consisting of our individual pasts and emotions related to that past; and a Collective Unconscious, which consists of the shared memories of all mankind. It is through the Collective Unconscious concept that you are going to analyze the drawings. The Collective Unconscious, according to Jung, is a universal memory that resides in each of our brains. That part of our brain is preprogrammed with memories and experiences of the history of all life on earth. This Collective Unconscious is reflected in the symbols that we use to describe our experiences (*Man and His Symbols,* 1964). The Collective Unconscious speaks in a symbol-system. If you understand this symbolic language, you can apply this language of symbols to the drawings and analyze them. The Collective Unconscious theory might sound unbelievable; however, Jung derived this idea through two lines of evidence. The first line comes from Jung's study of cultures from around the world and throughout history. In these diverse cultures, he found many cultures that never had direct experience or contact with one another, yet the same symbols appeared in the cultures representing the same things. One such symbol is the Mandala. In culture after culture, this symbol represents the interconnectedness of all life residing in the Self (see pgs. 121 and 122, *Brain Atlas*).

Christian stained glass

Tibetan Buddhist Mandalas

Ice crystals

Spider web

Navajo sand art

The other line of evidence that led Jung to the theory of a Collective Unconscious is the universal progression of drawing behavior in children. If each of us were able to go back and locate the first drawings we produced as a child, we would find the same pattern of drawing behavior. Everyone started with scribbles (Figure 1).

Then we started producing circular patterns, "Mandalas" (Figure 2).

Then we integrated the scribbles with the circular patterns, creating a representation of a person or some other symbol (Figure 3).

We produce what I call a Sun Ray Head, as seen in Figure 4. The common evolution of drawing is to then remove some of the rays and produce what I describe as M&M people, as illustrated in Figure 5. Finally, we develop our symbolic representation of a person through drawing.

Using the theory of the existence of a Collective Unconscious and an understanding of the language of Collective Unconscious, you will be able to analyze your drawings.

Initially, draw-a-figure-or-person tests were incorporated as a part of a test used to determine IQ in subjects. Florence Goodenough used drawings in this way in her *Measurement of Intelligence by Drawings* in 1926. John Buck (Buck, 1969; Buck and Warren, 1992) added the components of the house and tree.

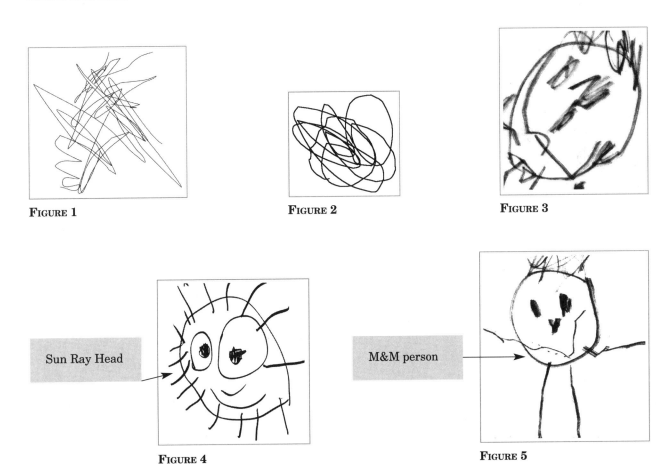

FIGURE 1

FIGURE 2

FIGURE 3

Sun Ray Head

FIGURE 4

M&M person

FIGURE 5

chapter **2**

Analysis of the House

What does the house possibly represent?_____

When looking at the house, look for themes with regard to: shelter, security, family, basic needs being met, love and attention needs being met, and how people relate to one another in the house. This is a glimpse into the past. Remember, what is on the house is just as significant as what is not on the house. Also, the drawing is a wish—not necessarily a wish as to how the past should have been, but a wish as to how it will be viewed by others.

Anything on the house that makes it more difficult for the artist/ anyone to look into or get into is saying, "I don't think I want to look into or get into this house again, and I certainly don't want anyone else looking into it."

DOORS

First, does the house have a door? Does it have a doorknob (Figures 6 and 7)? What we call a house without a door or doorknob is a prison. Prison is not a fun place. Does it meet your security needs? Yes, that is what prison is all about. But, people are not happy in prison. So, when one hears, "I put a roof over your head and food on your table, so you'd better follow my rules or there is the door," he feels indebted, and his sense of self-worth is diminished.

Is this why we bring people into the world, to feed and house them? There is more needed and deserved. This is reflected in the bleakness of the houses.

If the door is around the side of the house, then the person has to put effort into getting in the house (Figure 8). If there are stairs leading up to the house, this also represents work people have to go through to get to know the artist (Figure 9). The artist loses out in life by making it so hard for people to get to know him or her. There are many wonderful people who may not be willing to put out the time and energy to get beyond the obstacles and get to know the artist. Remember going Trick-or-Treating? We'd pass by all those houses with lots of stairs and houses where it looked like no one was home. It wasn't worth the effort.

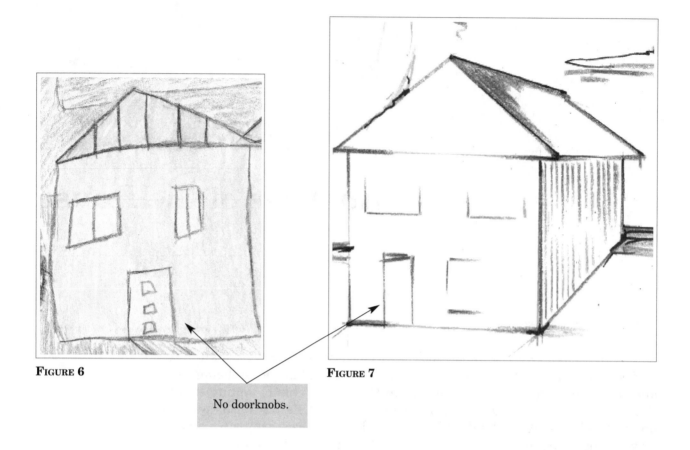

FIGURE 6

FIGURE 7

No doorknobs.

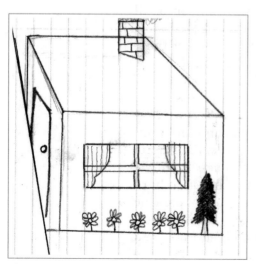

FIGURE 8

FIGURE 9

WINDOWS

Does the house have any windows? If it does, this is demonstrating that the artist is willing to look into his or her past. Are the windows on the second story? Are they above the door line, or are the windows level with the door (Figures 10 and 11)? Windows only above the door line again represent a past that someone must work to look into. One has to go get a ladder to see what is going on inside

The house can also be too open, not providing enough security (Figure 12). This artist tells too much. She tells you things you shouldn't hear and don't need to hear; she needs to form deep relationships too quickly.

CURTAINS

Are there curtains (Figure 13)? Do we put curtains in windows to let light in or keep light out? This symbolizes, "I don't wish to look into the house, and I sure don't want anyone else looking in, either." The number of windows can also be representational of the number of people in the house. Some windows can be more closed than others, meaning certain family members are more emotionally closed than others (Figures 14 and 15).

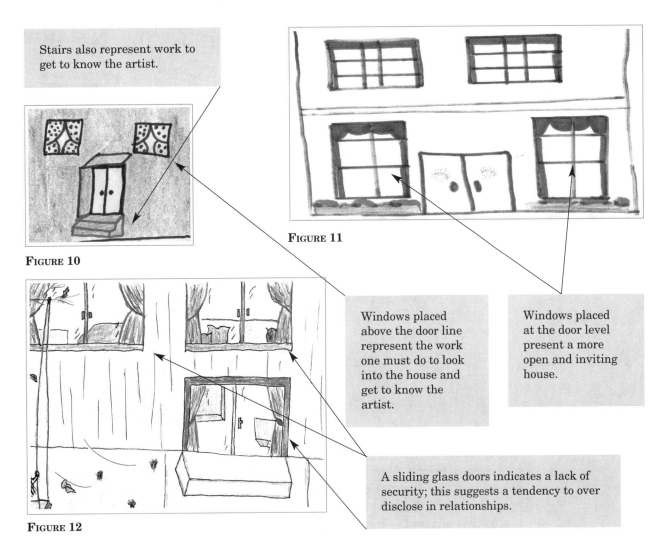

Stairs also represent work to get to know the artist.

FIGURE 10

FIGURE 11

Windows placed above the door line represent the work one must do to look into the house and get to know the artist.

Windows placed at the door level present a more open and inviting house.

A sliding glass doors indicates a lack of security; this suggests a tendency to over disclose in relationships.

FIGURE 12

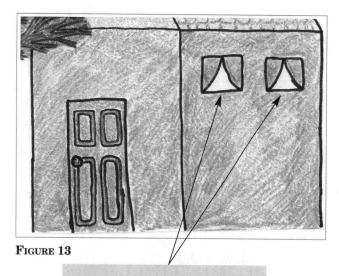

FIGURE 13

Windows obscured by curtains and around the side of house.

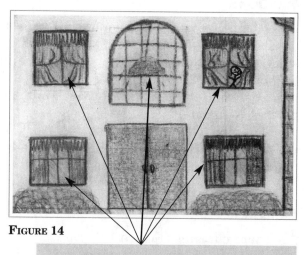

FIGURE 14

Windows obscured by curtains, different types and colors. *Note* **the center window is more "enlightened" than the others (family members).**

The number of windows may represent the number of family members and level of emotional openness of each.

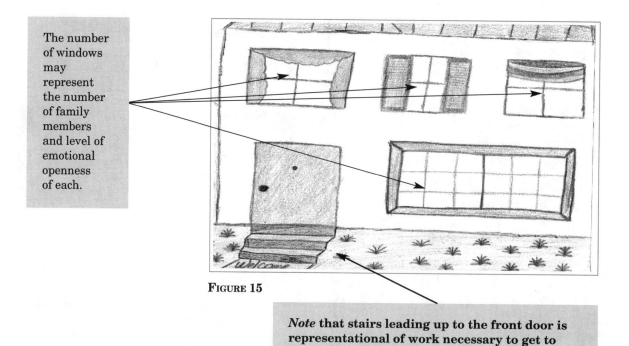

FIGURE 15

Note **that stairs leading up to the front door is representational of work necessary to get to know the artist.**

COLOR

The color of the house and parts of the house can have meaning if the artist had access to color when he or she produced the drawing. Red represents anger, and blue and pink represent the socialized male and female colors respectively. If there was access to color, and the artist chose predominately black, this suggests depression.

ROOFLINE

The amount of roofline is equal to the artist's awareness of his past life and life motives. If the roof area is small compared to the rest of the house, this is a person who has considerable self-awareness, although often very controlled. He wishes to be more spontaneous (Figures 16 and 18). If the roofline is large relative to the rest of the house, this means there is much the artist does not know about himself (Figures 17 and 19).

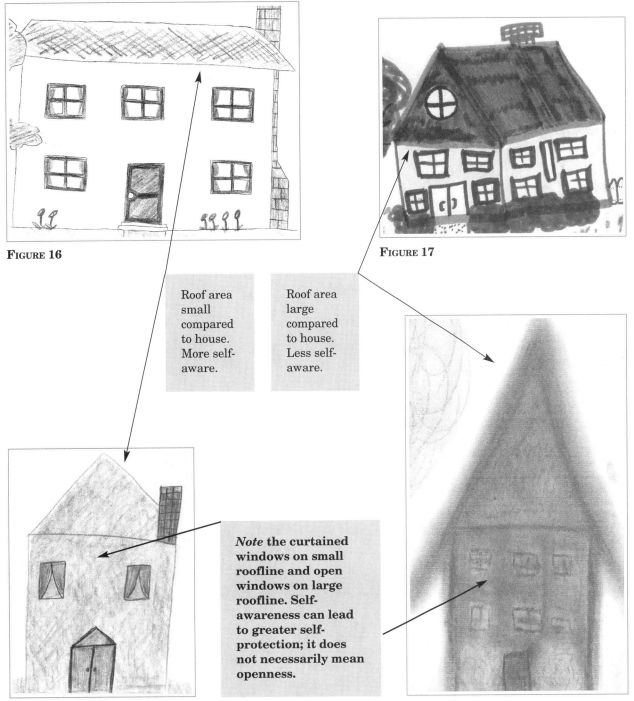

FIGURE 16

FIGURE 17

Roof area small compared to house. More self-aware.

Roof area large compared to house. Less self-aware.

Note the curtained windows on small roofline and open windows on large roofline. Self-awareness can lead to greater self-protection; it does not necessarily mean openness.

FIGURE 18

FIGURE 19

Window in Roofline

If there is a window in the roof area, this represents a person who is willing to look into the unknown and potential Pandora's Box that is one's unconscious mind (Figures 20 and 21).

Shingles

Are there shingles on the roof (Figures 22–24)? Is the artist a perfectionist? Perhaps he or she is a little obsessive. Perfectionism can be a good thing; the quality of a perfectionist's work is usually superior, but the burden of perfectionism is that the person only notices the flaws, not the greatness of the production. He or she notices the shingles out of alignment instead of

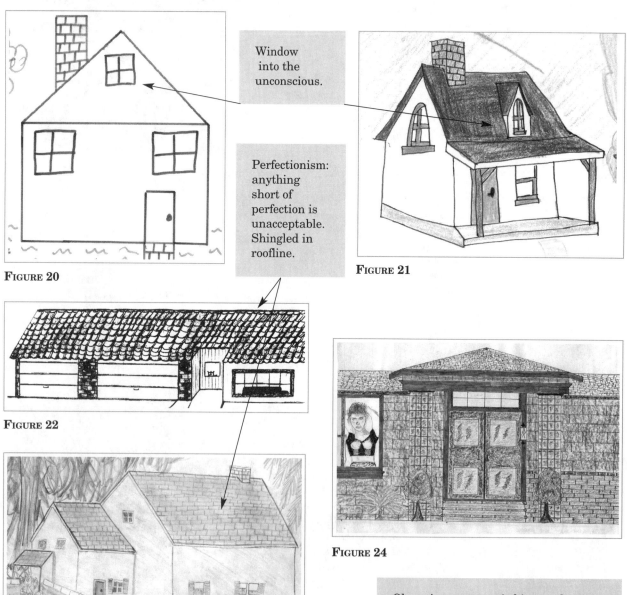

Window into the unconscious.

Perfectionism: anything short of perfection is unacceptable. Shingled in roofline.

Figure 20

Figure 21

Figure 22

Figure 23

Figure 24

Obsession: preoccupied intensely or abnormally; reflected in brickwork.

all the hard work that went into making the roof. Also, perfectionists often hate working with other people because their co-workers won't do it right. The perfectionist will have to do all the work. Perfectionism can become an issue when the person won't take on a project or activity if he or she can't complete it perfectly. Obsessions are not all bad; most everyone has a goal and pursues it with all of his or her energy. Obsessions become a problem when they interfere with all other activity, or when a person develops an "I can't live without you, and nobody else will either" mentality.

CHIMNEY

Does the drawing have a chimney? Is there smoke coming out of the chimney? Smoke symbolizes turmoil or conflict in the house (Figures 25–27). Remember the old saying, "Where there is *smoke,* there is fire?" Fire is an angry, destructive force. It doesn't care about the creatures of the forest. It burns Bambi's house and everything else in the way. That fire in your fireplace doesn't want to stay there. It wants to send out an ember and burn your whole house down. That is why we have screens in front of the fireplace. Fire contained represents warmth and passion; fire unconfined represents hatred.

House hellish in appearance. Fire leaping from windows.

Smoke representing turmoil. *Note* **the cut off house.**

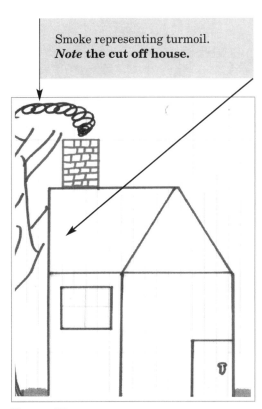

FIGURE 25

FIGURE 26

The person who drew the hellish house in Figure 26 wore a foot-high mohawk and had piercings and tattoos all over his body. When asked about his home life, he responded "It was Hell." In my experience, many people with foot-high mohawks have "issues." When one sees outlandish hair, one tends to stare. Often when these people with foot-high mohawks make eye contact, they respond with, "What the &%!$# are you looking at?" These are people just asking for a confrontation; their hair style choice is a billboard that says, "Just give me a reason. . . ." There are many people who have come from places that didn't meet their basic needs, so they are justifiably angry, but they turn this anger toward destructive purposes (see pg. 89, Self-esteem). Fortunately, the person who drew this picture saw himself as an artist and sculptor. This is a great metaphor, taking pieces of metal and melting them with fire in order to create art. Most people are very good at being destructive with their anger; few use it constructively. If the drawing has smoke coming out of the chimney, and the people in his house yelled, screamed, insulted, and disrespected one another, that artist knows how to relate this way. He is an expert in destructive skills, but he most likely doesn't know how to relate to people he loves in a healthy way. The chimney is also considered a phallic (anything resembling the male genitals) symbol and represents the father's influence in the home.

Note **all the smoke and nowhere to release the heat.** Father was a raging alcoholic.

Drawing from a 5-year-old boy referred to a hospital program after hitting a 2-year-old over the head with a Big Wheel.

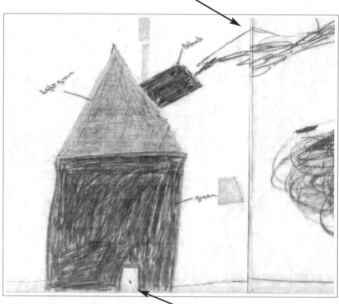

FIGURE 27

Note **the tiny door and no windows.**

House Placement

When there is only half a house on the paper, some of it is off the paper. This is often the production of a person coming from divorce. Half of that family unit is missing at any given time (Figures 28, 29).

No matter how a divorce is presented to a child, it is going to have a consequence. Even if the parents present it in the best way possible ("Mom and Dad no longer can live with each other, but they will always love you, and there was nothing you did to cause this situation."), there is a logical flaw. Why can't they live with each other? If they fell out of love with each other, they can fall out of love with the child. The parents may be able to explain why people fall out of love. However, divorced parents cannot explain how to stay in love, or they would not have divorced. This leads the child to doubt whether he or she is still loved in all his or her relationships, present and future. Children of divorce continually test their partner to see if the relationship is about to fail. Remember, this is what happens if the situation is ideally presented to the child. Most of the time, the parents are

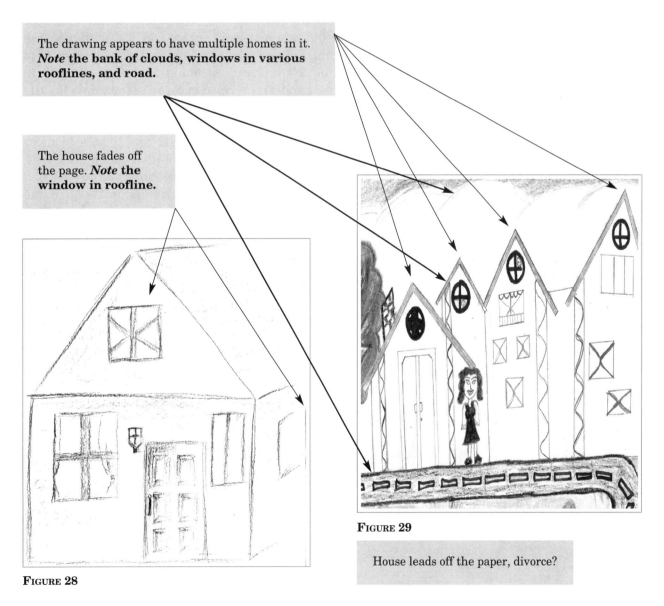

The drawing appears to have multiple homes in it. *Note* **the bank of clouds, windows in various rooflines, and road.**

The house fades off the page. *Note* **the window in roofline.**

FIGURE 28

FIGURE 29

House leads off the paper, divorce?

very angry and will call their ex-spouses all sorts of horrible things in the presence of the child. The child is used to relaying destructive messages from one parent to another and thus becomes the pipeline of all these angry feelings. The child becomes the center of the problem. Some parents will go to the extent of actually saying to the child, "I wouldn't have to deal with that so-and-so if it weren't for you." The child loves both parents at a deep fundamental level, and every time one parent insults the other parent, it puts down the child. This can have the consequence of the child then seeking out "lazy, worthless, and dumb" individuals to have relationships with as adults because he or she loved the "lazy, worthless, and dumb" (his or her parents). First-generation children who have emigrated from their country of origin will also draw half a house, reflecting the confusion of dealing with two different cultures.

VARIATIONS OF HOUSES

The house that is floating reflects an unstable home, usually an "—aholic" (workaholic, alcoholic, drugaholic) (Figure 30). These are escapisms that put the burden of feeling on outside sources (Figure 31). The children are made responsible for the feelings of the parents. This is an unfair denial of the person's ability to be a child. He or she has enough trouble dealing with his or her own feelings, yet the child is forced to become responsible for the feelings of the mother or father or both. This instability is reflected in the child's being responsible for everyone else rather than himself or herself. Happiness is not possible when the child is anxious. The profile of most "—aholics" is not that of rage and anger, but rather of depression, sickness, and having passed out. "If you are not there for me because you are passed out, then who will be?" A client reported playing with his brothers in the backyard, and when they heard the garage door open, they would say, "Oh

FIGURE 30

FIGURE 31

@&*%, Dad's home." They never knew who would come in the door, drunk dad who was happy, drunk dad who was angry, sober dad who was happy, sober dad who was angry, etc. The result is instability. Moody people are abusing others. The moody person asks others to be responsible for his upset feelings, and he does so in a dishonest manner. He doesn't make an announcement that he is in a bad mood so everyone has a chance to clear out of the room. He waits until someone does something to upset him, and then he directs his anger at him or her. After the fact, he uses the excuse "I am in a bad mood, and you should know that that upsets me." Well, we all prefer to be around happy people, so we will attempt to leave the person in the bad mood. The dishonest moody person then says, "What? You are going to leave me all by myself? What about in 'sickness and in health?'" What the moody person wants is someone to sit right there next to him or her and not do anything that upsets him or her. In other words, he or she wants someone who really does not exist. Trying to exist and not exist at the same time is craziness and is impossible. Ideally, moody people need to get control of their feelings and stop making other people responsible for them. If moody people had to spend time with just themselves, they might snap out of their mood fast. But misery demands company. Any house that is drawn by an adult that is not level reflects unstable emotions (see pg. 127, Temperament).

ELABORATE HOUSES

The elaborate house reflects a wish for structure and stability. Sometimes, the house is a fortress expressing a need to be protected (Figure 32); other times the person can't contain the desire to be grounded, to experience stability in his or her life (Figure 33). A person that drew a very elaborate

Elaborate structure, paper unable to contain. Excessive need for stability and structure in life. *Note* **the person climbing highest phallic symbol. Is he trying to impress dad?**

FIGURE 32

Extremely guarded, strong need to be protected. If only Prince Charming would appear in the near future.

FIGURE 33

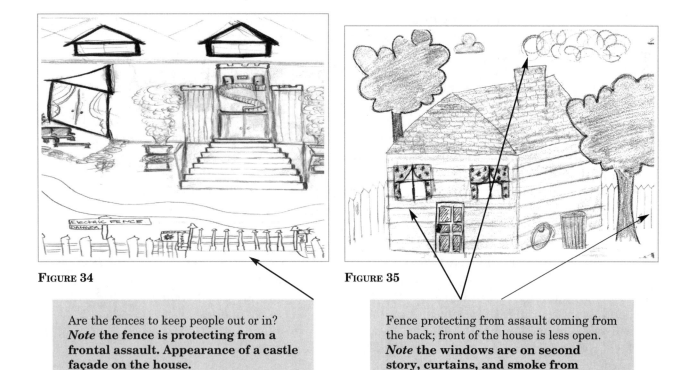

FIGURE 34

FIGURE 35

Are the fences to keep people out or in?
Note **the fence is protecting from a frontal assault. Appearance of a castle façade on the house.**

Fence protecting from assault coming from the back; front of the house is less open. *Note* **the windows are on second story, curtains, and smoke from chimney.**

structure that spilled off the paper reported she had a history of moving constantly as a child because of her father's military service. She reported how painful this was as a child with all the loss issues, making friends only to lose them again and again. It got to the point where she consciously decided not to form meaningful relationships. She said that she never wanted to put her children through this, and her wish was to have a big house and live in it forever. The caution to the dream is that she never experienced stability in her life. Will she be able to tolerate it, or will she decide she needs a constantly bigger and bigger house? Will she get to spend any time in the house with the people she wants to share it with? Or will she be too busy working trying to pay the mortgage on that big house?

GUARDED HOUSE

A guarded house with a fence around it reflects a need to be protected. The artist of such a house will have trouble having deep, meaningful relationships if he or she is unable to make himself or herself vulnerable (Figures 34 and 35). To love is to risk heartbreak. People who say, "I'll never open myself up like that again because it hurt too much" are denying themselves what defines our humanity, and this guarantees relationships that will be less fulfilling. The artist whose drawing is fenced in received the

FIGURE 36   **FIGURE 37**

Primitive Structures: To be contrasted with elaborate or guarded structures, they reflect minimal comfort, security, and stability in one's early life.

message from his or her family that, "You need to be protected and we don't think you can take care of yourself." The result of having received this message is a sense of inadequacy that has developed in the artist. Primitive houses provide little protection; the people must be self-reliant (Figures 36 and 37).

GARAGE

A garage represents a desire for freedom or escape (Figures 38 and 39). The garage contains the car that provides this opportunity. Obtaining a driver's license is a milestone. It is the first time in a person's life that he or she truly has a taste of freedom; he or she could just get in the car and go. People despise and become very angry when other people criticize their driving because it is more than the motor skill of driving that is being criticized, but what it symbolically represents: the person's freedom. The person criticizing the driver is criticizing and restricting the driver's expression of his or her freedom by making comments such as "Slow down!" or "Look out!" This is also why people won't admit they are intoxicated, for it is an admission of being out of control (see pg. 99, Annoyance).

FIGURE 38

The artist is symbolically expressing his anger at the family for setting the goals for the child and in essence infantilizing him. *Note* **the child is pulling his own wish/goal to have freedom out of the garage. Also, note dictation of the word smoke.**

Note **the tree is touching the house and is fenced in. The tree is lifeless.**

FIGURE 39

Here the person is ready to get into the car and seek his freedom.

chapter 3

Analysis of the Person

What does the person possibly represent? _____

In general, the person represents the artist's self-conception; the drawing is a picture of the artist in the present. Again, what is on the person and what is not on the person are equally significant.

FACIAL FEATURES

First, does the person have a face with facial features, or is the face obscured or not defined? In response to drawing a picture of a house, tree, and a person, one artist produced a drawing of a cardboard box with a ghost-like, ill-defined creature in it (Figure 40). What does a cardboard box provide? The barest minimum protection? If a person came from the equivalent

Ghost-like outline of person sheltered and nurtured by the equivalent of a cardboard box. *Note* the **appearance of two naked figures trying to warm and comfort each other.**

FIGURE 40

Faceless family and dog.

FIGURE 41

FIGURE 42

Faceless person and house. *Note* **half a house and similar empty appearance.**

Another faceless family and dog. *Note* **how the path leading to the door of the house becomes the door, giving the appearance that the house's contents are draining away.**

FIGURE 43

of a cardboard box, then just feeling safe in this world is comparable to scaling Mount Everest. Trying to figure out who one is and what one likes about oneself would be equivalent to striving for the moon and the stars (see pg. 89, Self-Esteem).

A person with no facial features reflects a lack of self-definition (Figures 41–43). This symbolizes a wish to be anonymous in terms of relationships with others, reflecting a lack of connection to both the self and others. The lack of features is not due to oversight or lack of drawing skill. The artist has chosen to leave the faces blank.

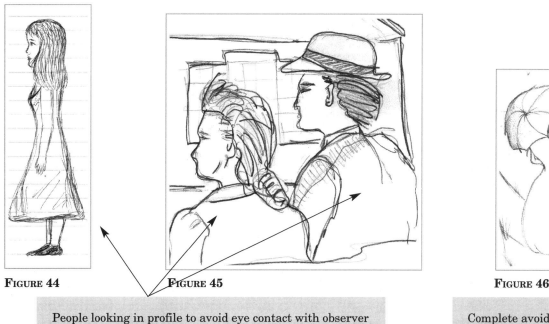

FIGURE 44   **FIGURE 45**   **FIGURE 46**

People looking in profile to avoid eye contact with observer in attempt to protect self.

Complete avoidance of contact. *Note* **that even bunny doesn't want to make eye contact.**

EYES

The next critical feature of the person is the eyes. Are the eyes looking out of the paper at whoever is looking at the picture? Or are they looking away or in profile? Recall the saying, "Eyes are the window to the soul." If the person is not making contact with the observer, the person is unable or un-willing to make contact with others (Figures 44–46). He or she will not allow others to connect with his or her soul (self).

The person has experienced too much pain with past contacts, so he or she wishes not to experience it again. Some artists and readers may re-member hearing this as a child, "Look at me when I am talking to you. If you ever do that again, I'll . . . ." Eye contact was demanded of the child, and then what came raining down on him or her was punishment and pain. So he or she may have broken eye contact and distracted himself or herself by humming, but the rhythm and cadence of language is recognized by the person; and when the lecturer paused, the child looked up and said, "Yes Sir/Yes Mama." Even dogs know about eye contact. Doggy Psychology 101: the first dog to break eye contact is the one saying "You are not a threat." When a dog owner tells his dog to do something and the dog looks at the owner and then just looks away, the dog is testing the owner's ability to control it. If a picture doesn't have eyes looking out of the paper, then the artist is already broken. When we see homeless people asking for spare change, do we generally make eye contact and say, "I am really sorry about your plight, but I am a little short myself" or maybe, "What is wrong with you? Why don't you get a job?" No, we usually just walk by, making no eye contact, ignoring the person. Why don't we make eye contact? Because it is painful! It is too real an illustration of "There, but for the grace of God go I." Another situation regarding eye contact and its importance is with the example of a person who makes eye contact but then chooses to ignore the person with whom he or she made eye contact. Many of us have had the experience of walking through a public place, such as a mall, and seeing someone from our past. But we choose not to acknowledge him or her with a comment or a nod of the head or the universal human acknowledgement of another, the eyebrow raise. We just make fleeting eye contact and keep walking. If any of us parachuted into the most remote area of the rainforest where the indigenous people have never seen anything like us before and know nothing of our kind, those indigenous people would at least give us the universal eyebrow raise. But we won't give this to this person from our past. As we walk away from that person whom we failed to acknowledge, we then start thinking about him or her and who he or she is and how we can't believe we encountered that person. As we continue walking, we keep obsessing about him or her. If we had said something to him or her or raised our eyebrow, we would not even be giving him or her a second thought. Why are we doing this? We are obsessively repeating thoughts about him or her to try to distract ourselves from acknowledging some part of our past. We are trying to forget a time, a place, or a person who once was part of our life. We are saying to ourselves, "I can't believe I was like him in my past." We are mentally trying to put a whole bunch of shingles on our house (past) (Figures 47 and 50). That person we are trying to deny is part of us. If we continue to deny our past, it will forever affect and direct our lives. It is necessary to acknowledge one's past in order to come to some understanding.

The artist who draws figures avoiding eye contact has trouble accepting compliments (Figures 48 and 49). He assumes that the person paying him a compliment is trying to manipulate him. Or the person is not aware that the artist feels he is undeserving of the compliment. The person giving the compliment is saying things that the artist can't say to himself, so he can't tolerate hearing them. The artist reacts to the compliment by rejecting it.

FIGURE 47

FIGURE 48

FIGURE 49

FIGURE 50

Avoidance of eye contact in person and obsessive capacities reflected in shingles.

In a hospital program for emotionally disturbed children, a boy produced a disturbing drawing (Figure 51). When told "That's really good," he immediately crumpled up the picture and threw it on the floor. The boy could not tolerate the positive message. For eight years, this boy had received the message that he was not good, that something was wrong with him, that he acted evil. Does the Devil do good work? Certainly not! He had two choices when he received a compliment: 1) Accept the compliment and discount every message he received for his first 8 years of life; or 2) Destroy the evidence of his goodness. Many people have gotten out of a relationship because their partner was too nice. That is because, like this boy, some people can't tolerate the positive message, so they destroy the evidence of their niceness, crumpling up the relationship and throwing it away. How did I attempt to help this boy? I picked up his drawing and said, "I am scared; I don't really want to see the picture." I then uncrumpled the drawing, mocked horror, and threw it down. The boy then got up, picked up the picture, and said, "Look at it." I said "No." The boy then proceeded to follow me around the room trying to get me to look at his picture. I then challenged him and the rest of the children in the group. I bet they could not draw a scarier picture. Immediately the children were drawing (Figure 52), and the boy further smoothed out his drawing and

Figure 51

Drawing of "Pit of Hell" and devil. *Note* **this is not a "good" drawing in subject or at a developmental level.**

Figure 52

Drawing produced by different child in response to challenge. *Note* **the drawing is developmentally much better, child same age, illustrating other child's work is not "good."**

said, "We will put Paul in the Pit of Hell." The boy went from a destructive process, crumpling up his work, to a constructive one of making more pictures.

The minds of Stephen King, Clive Barker, and Wes Craven must be scary, disturbing places to come up with their collective material. However, they are good scary constructive places as opposed to the bad scary destructive places of a Jeffery Dalhmer or other serial killers. What does this story mean for those who draw a person who is looking away? If one wants to have relationships without unhealthy levels of stress, which are good for his or her self-image, then he or she is going to have to stress and challenge himself or herself to put up with nice relationships, even though it feels uncomfortable to affirm "I deserve this." Eventually, getting to a place where one can say, "I demand nice people in my life, and I don't want people who can't act nice in my life," is needed.

HANDS

Does the person have hands; or are the hands withdrawn, behind the body, or occupied by holding something? If the figure has no hands, this symbolizes a lack of connection to others (Figures 53 and 54). It may also symbolize impulsiveness on the part of the artist, not taking the time necessary to draw the hands. Either reason for not having hands will have the same consequence: limited depth in relationships. Remember, these drawings are wishes, and the artist who makes figures without hands wishes he or she did not have to make a connection. Connections in the past have been

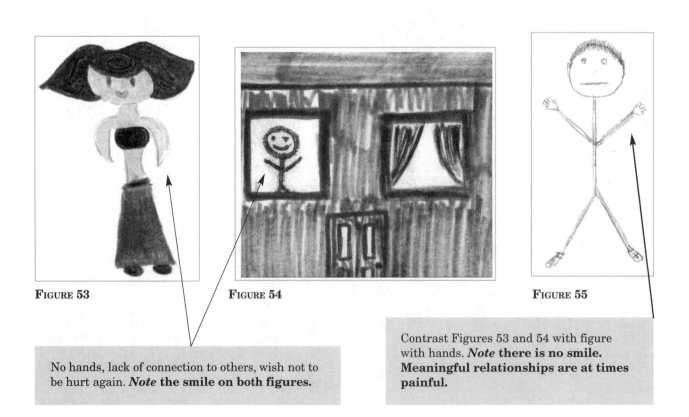

FIGURE 53   **FIGURE 54**   **FIGURE 55**

No hands, lack of connection to others, wish not to be hurt again. *Note* **the smile on both figures.**

Contrast Figures 53 and 54 with figure with hands. *Note* **there is no smile. Meaningful relationships are at times painful.**

painful. Someone in the past emotionally slapped the artist when he or she made a connection. To avoid future pain, the artist makes it impossible to connect with him or her.

What do babies do with their hands? They first grasp; then they crawl around using their hands to connect with the world. They pick up objects, then put the object in their mouths. This represents connecting with and then consuming the world. What do people do when they meet? They shake hands. This tradition came from a defensive gesture demonstrating that neither party had a weapon in his hand. In the drawing, the handless person won't even show his or her hand; he or she is guarded. The artist might claim she forgot to put on hands. To this, Freud would say "exactly" (but, he would say it in German). Others claim that hands are difficult things to draw, so they did not try to. A logical interpretation of this claim is the connection has to be perfect before that person will attempt it. Human connections are never perfect. The impulsive or hyperactive person who didn't take time to draw hands will suffer consequences. Meaningful relationships take time to develop (Figure 55), and if one is quickly and impulsively moving in and out of people's lives, any connections he or she makes will be superficial (see pg. 115, ADHD).

The person who has something in her hands is trying to distract and make excuses for not connecting with others (Figure 56). The stance of the figure is also significant. A significant portion of our communication with others is nonverbal, coming from our body language. Crossed arms on the figure symbolize one who is closed off and protective (Figures 57 and 58). The arms raised signify submission or having given up (Figures 59–61).

Figure 56

Figure 57   **Figure 58**

Hand occupied and withdrawn, representing fear of connection. ***Note* the similar military stance, at attention.**

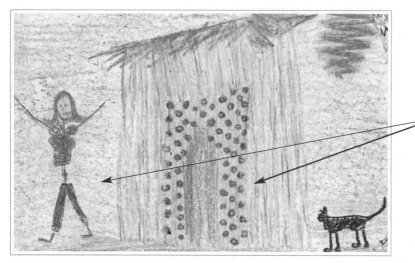

Vulnerable, submissive pose of figure with no hands. *Note* **the primitive house where few needs were met.**

FIGURE 59

Lovers with no way to make a connection, since none has any hands. *Note* **that both couples are on unstable ground.**

FIGURE 60   FIGURE 61

FEET

If the figure is lacking feet, this signifies that the artist feels stuck in some aspect of his or her life: stuck in a bad family, a bad relationship, a bad job, a bad station in life, or just a bad life (Figures 62–65). Not only is he or she stuck, but he or she is also unequipped to change anything in his or her lives. Typically, having no hands goes along with having no feet. Since relationships are the foundation of all lives, then these stuck and unconnected people lack that very foundation (see pg. 105, Stress Explanation).

In response to being asked to draw a picture of herself with her mother, a 4-year-old child produced the drawing in Figure 66.

What does this look like? A blob, an amoeba, a whale, a giant universe, a nothing! One might suspect that there is some neurological problem that inhibits the child's ability to draw. This was not the case. When asked to draw other people, the child was able to produce the M&M and lollipop

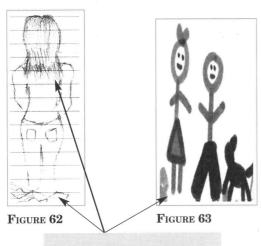

FIGURE 62   **FIGURE 63**

No feet, sense of being
stuck in one's life. *Note*
the lack of eye contact.

FIGURE 64

No anything, face,
hands or feet.

FIGURE 65

No anything
person and cat.

FIGURE 66

Ill-defined scribbling representing mother and self. Drawn by 4-year-old. *Note* **the shape of border
(see Figure 68).**

Drawing by same girl of another child.
Note: **The skill level is much higher on peer drawing than on family/self portrait.**

FIGURE 67

people (Figure 67). What could account for the difference between the self-drawing and the drawing of a peer? The history on this child is that the mother was a disturbed transient.

The mother was still breast feeding this child at age 4, and she carried the child around everywhere she went. The mother treated the child like an infant. When told that this was not "normal" behavior, the mother said, "You know, you are probably right. I probably should have gotten a dog instead." This comment illustrates the level of connection the mother had to the child. Why do we like dogs so much? Because they are baby-like, dogs are dependent on us to meet their needs for their entire lifetime. With this child, the state stepped in and put the child in foster care. The mother and child received counseling. In a short period of time, the child produced the drawing of herself and mother shown in Figure 68.

Infants have no sense of self; they are the whole world. If they need something, they cry, and the world, hopefully, jumps to meet those needs. This child, who was being treated like an infant, had no opportunity to develop a sense of self, so she was unable to differentiate herself from her mother. She could only produce a giant blob/universe. As she started to experience a sense of self in the therapy and foster care, she could then reflect this in her drawings, forming a Mandala. Ultimately, the mother was unable to develop her parental skills enough to take care of her daughter.

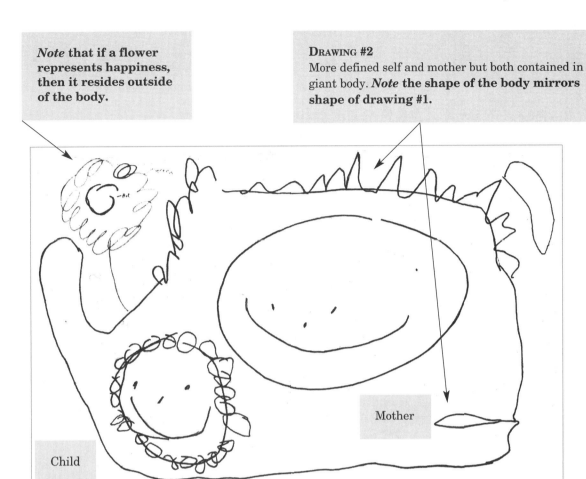

FIGURE 68

Parental rights were severed, and the child was then put into permanent foster care. A short period of time after that, she produced the picture shown in Figure 69.

This child is not saying to herself while drawing picture #1, "I have an amoebic, one-celled universal relationship with my mother, so I draw this." She has not experienced a sense of self and has no identity separate from her mother, so she cannot reflect self-definition in her drawings. As she received more independence, a self emerged, and then she could reflect it in her drawings shown in Figures 68 and 69. Artists who draw face-less, arm-less, feet-less figures have not had enough of their basic needs met in order for them to experience a sense of self independent of their environment. Independence is too dangerous. The artist is worried about whether she is safe or whether anyone loves her. This obsessive worry leaves her no time to be concerned about who she is, whether she likes herself, and it leaves her with no energy to define herself (see pg. 89, Self-Esteem Explanation).

Child identified self: "That's me in the tree."

FIGURE 69

Note the foster mother is floating, relationships for child remain unstable.

Well-defined figures/self. *Note* the therapist's writing, directed by child to identify foster mother as "Grandma."

NOSES

In response to drawing a picture that included a person, one client drew a figure with no nose. I circled the space where the nose should have been and wrote "Drugs?" I knew the history of this client and knew that she had been in recovery for cocaine abuse. The client saw this, and she responded, "Oh, I thought I was over that." I explained that she would never be "over that." "That" was part of her past; the past she wanted to forget had brought her to this point in her life, and it was a past she could not just conveniently forget. Remember, these drawings are a wish, a bit of a dream; and this person wished she did not have to acknowledge the time when she had a problem, so she simply erased the evidence of it (colorplates 70, 71, and 73).

I knew a girl who at the age of eight started drawing herself without any nose on all her self-drawings. I don't believe she had a drug problem, but at the time she had a number of freckles on her nose and was often told, "How cute!" She hated the freckles, so she wished them away in her self-drawings. I was explaining the House, a Tree, and a Person to my classes one day and had just related the story of this girl when a student said "My son doesn't draw any noses on his figures." Being the therapist, I inquired as to the age of the child, and the student said her son was eight. I then asked, "Is there anything about his nose that is significant?" She responded, "Well, he is always picking his nose." I thought "Oh no." Here this child is amongst beasts because that is what 8-year-olds tend to be.

That is the age when personal body flaws are picked out by other the 8-year-olds. Whether one had glasses, was too short, too tall, too fat, too skinny, had buck teeth, talked with a lisp, had red hair, or any type of flaw, the beasts attacked the child like a pack of wolves and called him or her names to see how he or she would respond. If they called the flawed child a name, and the child attacked back with something clever like, "You're a poo-poo head," then the wolves were appeased. Seeing that the child could stand up for himself, the child was then allowed to join the group. This is part of the normal socialization process of children, though it is painful going through the process. However, if the child responded with, "I am going to tell the teacher," or if, heaven forbid, the child were to cry, he or she becomes a limping caribou and the wolves continue to attack unmercifully. This boy who drew himself with no nose was among beasts, and he was giving the wolves ammunition. He had marked himself as "The nose picker" or "Booger Boy." There had to be something psychological going on to account for this. I then asked the mother, "What is it about his nose?" She said, "He has a really big nose." Symbolically, what was he trying to do by picking his nose? Did he figure if he picks enough stuff out of his nose, it will collapse down on his face, thus creating a smaller nose? He wishes that his big nose weren't there. It's clearly not about mucous. I then asked the mother, "Whose nose is it like?" The mother then blurted out, "Mine, and I have always hated it." Is a big nose on a boy as big a deal as a big nose on a girl in our society? No, tremendous numbers of males aren't running out and having rhinoplasty and augmentation because they don't like their body image. It is quite possible the child could have gone through his entire life thinking nothing was flawed about his nose. If teased, it would have been about his big nose—not his nose picking—and he could have defended that; instead, his mother's self-consciousness became his, and this he is unable to defend. Most of our fears, phobias, and self-image issues did not originate with us (Colorplate 72), but from others who foisted their personal problems on us. This was the mother's issue, not the son's. But, now the past (the house) is dictating the present (the person). If one becomes more aware that the fears and concerns one has are not his or hers alone, it is easier to rid oneself of them.

PERSON PLACEMENT

Where the person is, relative to the house, is significant. If the person is in the house, is he in the house because he wants to stay there and feel secure, or is he trapped in the house (Colorplates 74–76)? If he is in the house because he feels secure there, and he has received messages that the world is a scary place and "we" will always take care of "you," then that person is receiving a message not about the world, but about his ability to function in the world independently. That message is that the people in the house don't feel the artist is capable of taking care of himself in the big, wild world. The message that "we" will always take care of "you" is a false one because those people won't always be there for the artist. After all, people die. When this occurs, the person who has always lived, and been taken care of, in the house will not be equipped to be independent. Therefore, he will end up seeking dependent relationships in the future. If the person is drawn trapped in the house, the artist is expressing a need to escape and a willingness to do anything to escape. In order to obtain his freedom, he will gravitate to any relationship that might offer freedom from the original family/house. The new relationship will also end up trapping and controlling him because freedom is so alien to him that any relationship that provides freedom is intolerable.

When drawings are made with people on top of the house trying to repair it, the artist should ask himself or herself, "Did I wreck the house? Is it my job to fix it?" A better plan would be to take that energy and go build a house just the way she wants. People rarely have the capabilities to repair a family or past, as symbolized by the house.

SIZE OF THE PERSON

The size of the person relative (perspective) to the house is significant in that it is communicating that the development of the person is more important or influential than the family at this time (Colorplates 77 and 78).

Here is a production by a person who tends toward narcissism (see pg. 93, Narcissism).

One would have trouble getting one's needs met or noticed in a relationship with the artist above. He has a grandiose sense of self-importance (Colorplate 79). Contrast this drawing with the person who is insignificant and dominated by the house (Colorplate 80).

chapter 4

Analysis of the Tree

What does the tree possibly represent? _____

The tree symbolically represents growth, possible paths of life, and a future picture. The house is representative of the past, the person is the present, and the tree will be a guide to the future. If the artist has a secure house that is open and stable, he or she will typically have a well-defined person and a positive future outlook. If the artist came from a bleak, unstable home, he or she will have an ill-defined person and a negative future picture. The individual who drew a cardboard box for the house has a ghostly undefined self and drew a potted plant for the tree. However, for most of those who came from the equivalent of a cardboard box, it wouldn't even occur to them to include a plant, even one without leaves.

LEAVES

The first question to ask is does the tree have any leaves? If a tree doesn't have any leaves, it begs the question, "Is it dormant or is it dead?" (Colorplates 81, 82 and 84). If it is dormant, what are the necessary conditions for the future to allow the plant to blossom and leaf out, and when is that going to happen? If it is dead, this is a very negative future picture. The artist might say, "I drew the picture in fall, and all the trees are losing or have lost their leaves." Remember, no one was asked to draw a tree in fall; he or she chose to draw the tree in fall. Something about a bleak, lifeless tree in fall resonates with the artist. If the house is open, stable, and secure, the tree will have leaves representing a future with growth and potential (Colorplate 83).

BRANCHES

If there are leaves in the tree, then are there also branches in the tree? These represent paths the artist can travel in life. If there is no branching in the tree, the artist's chosen path is unclear, as is his or her future (Colorplates 86, 87, and 91).

Fruit and Nest

Fruit in the tree represents rewards that are obtainable in the future (Colorplates 83–86). The lack of fruit does not necessarily mean that there are no rewards in the future, but it demonstrates that the future rewards are unclear. Fruit on the ground represents either obtained goals or missed opportunities.

A nest in the tree symbolizes that the goal of having a family is significant to the artist.

Hole in Trunk

Is there a hole in the trunk of the tree? If there is, then this represents loss (Colorplates 86, 89–93). The hole is saying, "As the person was traveling the path of life, he lost something or somebody significant." The artist is not as equipped as he would like to be to deal with life if he had not experienced this loss (see pg. 105, Stress).

The loss could be a person significant to the artist, a divorced family, a loss of a relationship, even a favorite pet. Why does a hole represent loss? If a person were to go to a real forest, the holes in the trunks are rot, and those trees are not as healthy as ones without holes. It can also represent that a path one might pursue has been removed.

Sometimes the hole will be filled with a creature. An owl, a bird, or a squirrel will be put in the hole filling up the void (Colorplates 94–96). What do these creatures represent? An owl symbolically represents wisdom. The artist is saying, "I lost something, but I gained wisdom." The bird represents a desire to fly away from the loss. A bird in a nest represents a wish to create a new life in response to the loss. A squirrel says, "I lost something, and I have gone squirrelly/nuts!"

Differently Shaped Trees

Trees that have a cloud-like appearance suggest that the future is cloudy and may just float away (Colorplates 97–98).

Trees that are mushroom cloud in appearance suggest that the future is volatile and could explode at any time (Colorplates 99–100).

Trees of Varied Type

Trees drawn to look like pine trees or Christmas trees are conveying that the person's future and goals are focused in one direction (Colorplates 101–103). This is not a bad thing, but there is a caution that if that specific goal is not obtained, every other goal is at a lower level. The person may end up in a world of regret, saying to him or herself, "If I had only done so-and-so, I wouldn't be here."

Trees drawn to look like palm trees represent a future marked by dreams and escapism (Colorplates 104–106). The odds of obtaining this future are slim given the person's current position in the world; he or she is dreaming of winning a lottery. Palm trees are also drawn by people with very high aspirations or goals, and the rewards are great if they obtain these goals, signified by the coconuts. However, the path to these goals/rewards is long and has few fruits of labor along that path. The trunk of a coconut tree is long, hard to climb, and often covered by spikes.

TREE TOUCHING HOUSE

If the tree is touching the house, family and goals are tied together (Figures 107–109). Having the family or past as a direct influence on one's goals is not necessarily a bad thing if they are mutually arrived upon goals. If the goals have been imposed upon the person, this can lead to disaster. The people in the house are attempting to live vicariously through the child. The child will always end up disappointing the parents for a number of reasons. First, it is never as satisfying when another person achieves something that another family member personally wanted to achieve. This will lead to the parent criticizing the child no matter what he or she has achieved, because the parent was not the one who achieved it. Second, the child will not be as motivated as he or she would have been if he or she had set the goal, and will not obtain any personal satisfaction from achieving the goal because it was never his or hers in the first place. The classic example is the little league parent or stage parent who is constantly yelling at the child for striking out or missing a goal or not getting the part, never noting the good catch, nice pass, or good audition. The parent becomes a source of embarrassment to the child by inappropriately blaming and raging against those who the parent believes interfered with his or her child's achievement. The parent is always yelling at coaches, umpires, teachers, and other children on the team.

Sometimes the artist will actually put the house in the tree. This symbolizes that the family and goals are intimately tied together, if not inseparable. The artist who places the house in the tree feels trapped. If the artist goes against the wishes of the family, he risks the disappointment of the family or even complete rejection. All these pictures of houses in trees have a ladder or rope to help the person climb up (Colorplates 110–113). This represents the help and sacrifice the family has provided or will provide to the person to reach the family's goals. The sacrifices of the family borders on martyrdom, which further adds to the guilt of the person who fails to obtain the family goals (see pg. 67, Freud Primer).

OTHER OBJECTS IN TREE

If there is a swing or tire swing in the tree, this is symbolic of someone who wants a break from his or her goal path by taking a vacation (Colorplates 114–118). It can also represent people who are distracting themselves from their goal path. The more leisure time a person has is not related to how happy a person is; in fact, the opposite has been found to be true. Doing meaningful work has the greatest relationship to happiness.

PERSON RELATIVE TO TREE

Where the person is positioned relative to the tree is also significant (Colorplates 119–123). If the person is lying up against the tree, this represents the person who is trying to gain enough strength or courage to start along his or her path of life, or he or she may be undecided as to what course he or she should take. If the tree is bleak, representing a bleak future (trees with no leaves), then the person is resigning himself or herself to that future and figuring "what's the use" of climbing that tree. The person engaged in an activity, such as reading, is someone who is distracting himself or herself from the immediate goals.

chapter 5

Objects Peripheral to Drawing

BIRDS

Birds represent the desire for freedom, to break the bounds of the earth (Colorplates 124–125). The person wishes to fly away from his or her problems.

CLOUDS AND RAIN

Clouds in the sky represent depression (Colorplates 126–127). The old saying "When it rains, it pours" applies to clouds in drawings. The people living in the areas of the earth that receive the least amount of sunlight during the winter months exhibit the greatest amount of depression. This disorder is called Seasonal Affective Disorder. People can suffer from greater or lesser amounts of depression. Depression can have multiple causes: environmental, genetic, or a combination of both.

SUN

The sun represents the father's influence on the artist beyond the house (past) into the present (Colorplates 128–131). Having a sun in the picture does not necessarily have a positive or negative connotation, just that the father is influential. However, the sun can represent an overwhelming influence if it is very large in relation to the rest of the objects in the drawing. Clouds around the sun symbolize the father has some depression.

MOON

The moon represents the mother's influence beyond the house (past) into the present. As with the sun, having a moon in the picture does not necessarily mean the mother has a positive or negative connotation, just that she is influential in the artist's current life (Colorplates 132–133).

MAILBOXES

Mailboxes represent that the artist is waiting for some information about his or her future (Colorplates 134–135). The artist engages in a passive process of obtaining the information, rather than actively seeking it out. His or her future hinges on this information.

No-nose, No-hands, No-feet couple. ***Note*** **the hypnotic swirl pattern everywhere, and very psychedelic in appearance.**

No-nose, No-hands, No-feet person. Disconnect from all of her body. ***Note*** **the angel appearance to body; wish to fly away to a more heavenly place.**

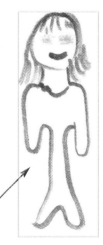

COLORPLATE 70

COLORPLATE 71

No-nose, No-hands, No-feet person drawn with the burden of a brick house in her life. This symbolizes a tremendous need for security.

FIGURE 72

COLORPLATE 73

The person *in* the house may feel more secure, but at the same time controlled and trapped. He is receiving messages about his inability to take care of themselves. ***Note*** **that the person in this house is gray while the rest of the house is colored red; smoke is also gray which represents anger over being trapped. The color of the house is red, an angry color. The curtains are blue, (socialized male color) male controlling household.**

COLORPLATE 74

COLORPLATE 75

COLORPLATE **76**

Person busy repairing house she didn't break. ***Note* the neglected-trapped child in house. The prominent garage, a symbol of a desire to escape, contains a car that allows for freedom.**

COLORPLATE **77**

COLORPLATE **78**

The houses are insignificant compared to the person. The person is the focus of all the attention. Extreme differences in size, as seen here, border on complete self-absorption.

COLORPLATE 79

The drawing is saying, "I am the whole world."

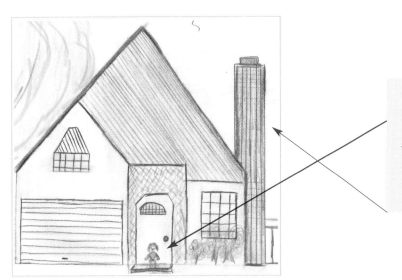

COLORPLATE 80

The person is insignificant compared to house, reflecting diminished sense of self-worth. *Note* **the person doesn't even reach the doorknob.** Chimney large, representing dominating father (phallic symbol).

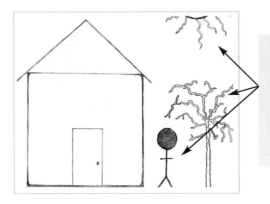

Note the lifeless trees and ill-defined person. House's minimal capacity to meet needs. Branches = sun rays

COLORPLATE 81

COLORPLATE 82

Stunted, depressed trees come from bleak depressing houses and hopelessness.

Contrast tree with leaves and fruit with tree with falling leaves and trapped person.

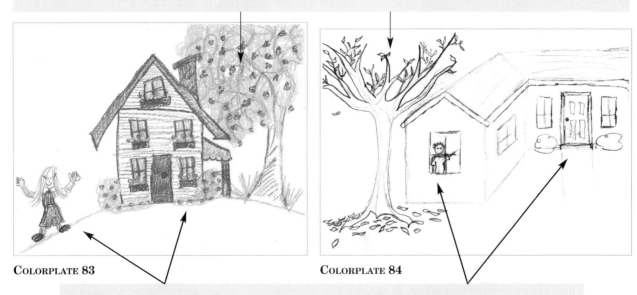

COLORPLATE 83

COLORPLATE 84

Note: **Compare open house with the claustrophobic house and the colorful open free person with closed-up gray person. Note the distance to escape door.**

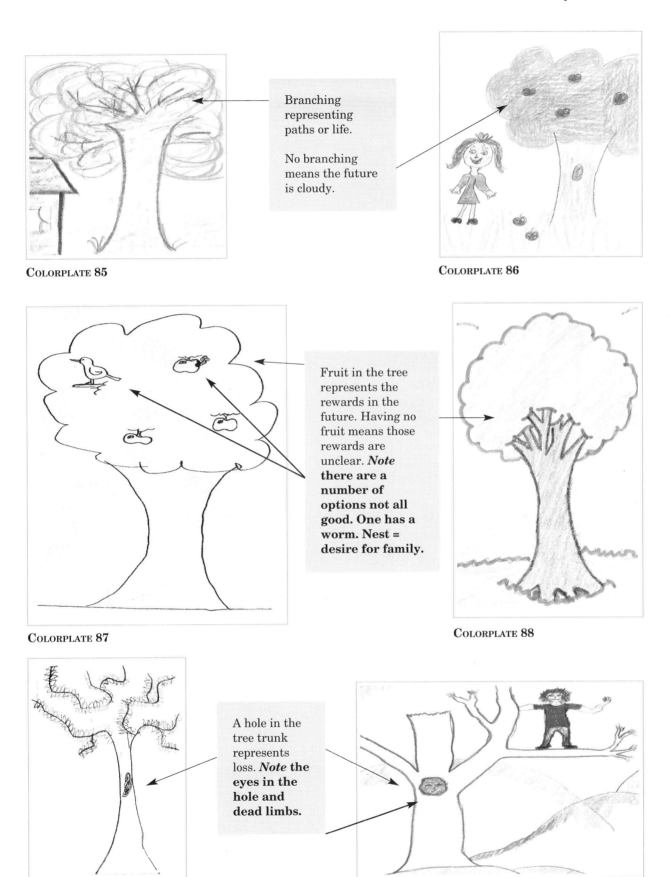

COLORPLATE 85

COLORPLATE 86

Branching representing paths or life.

No branching means the future is cloudy.

COLORPLATE 87

COLORPLATE 88

Fruit in the tree represents the rewards in the future. Having no fruit means those rewards are unclear. *Note* **there are a number of options not all good. One has a worm. Nest = desire for family.**

A hole in the tree trunk represents loss. *Note* **the eyes in the hole and dead limbs.**

COLORPLATE 89

COLORPLATE 90

COLORPLATE 91

Loss results in loss of identity. *Note* **there is no face on person.**

COLORPLATE 92

Loss results in person being stuck and disconnected. *Note* **there are no hands or feet.**

COLORPLATE 93

Loss results in complete disconnect from world. *Note* **the eyes are closed; pose of tree matches person and looks like someone putting hands up just before being arrested. Same pose as tree in Colorplate 92.**

COLORPLATE 94

Owl or nesting bird: Lost something and gained wisdom or wish to create a new life.

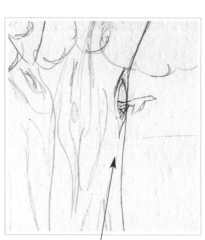

COLORPLATE 95

Bird: Lost something and wish to escape and be free of the loss.

COLORPLATE 96

Squirrel: Lost something and has gone "nuts."

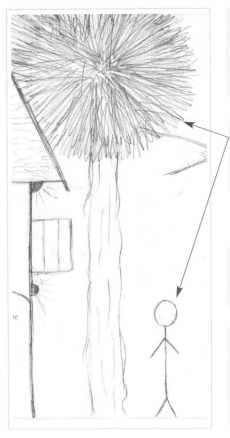

Tree has the appearance of a dandelion. The future could blow away in the wind.

Note the person is undefined, as is the future.

Note the tree top and cloud identical in shape.

A tree with a cloud-like appearance says the future could just float away. *Note* **the hole in trunk.**

COLORPLATE 97

COLORPLATE 98

Trees presenting explosive looking futures.

COLORPLATE 99

COLORPLATE 100

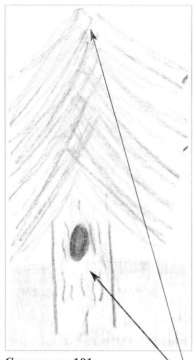

COLORPLATE 101

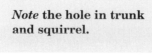

Note the hole in trunk and squirrel.

COLORPLATE 102

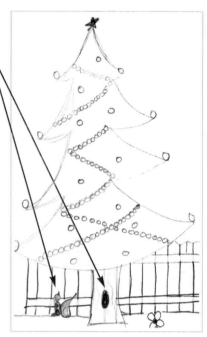

COLORPLATE 103

Pines represent focused life path. *Note* the loss. Top of tree off the paper, representing lofty goals that are perhaps unobtainable.

Note the faint roots implying path was set very early in life.

Christmas tree, goals are focused and if person gets to top, he is a star, if not, a loser?

COLORPLATE 104

COLORPLATE 105

High aspirations for the future. *Note* the figures lack hands or feet.

Palm trees = fantasies about future.

Note the spiky path.

COLORPLATE 106

COLORPLATE **107**

House and tree touching, so the past is dictating the future. *Note* **the house tilted toward tree. Chimney representational of father tilted the most.**

COLORPLATE **108**

House is literally growing the future. *Note* **the chimney representational of father who is deciding person's goals, house is a garage which equals freedom.**

COLORPLATE **109**

The future represented by the tree crushes the house/family. The drawing is saying, "If I disclose my goals and future, it will crush my family." *Note* **the person is a passive observer.**

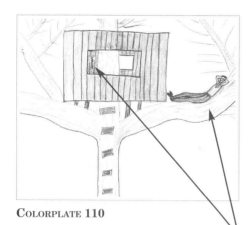

COLORPLATE 110

Tree and house are one. *Note* **the pennant says Harvard, yet the pose of person is relaxed (passive resistance directed against family).**

COLORPLATE 111

Note the primitive structure where few needs are met beyond those necessary to meet goals. Loss signified by hole.

COLORPLATE 112

This elaborate structure in the tree is still being worked on. *Note* **the second house in background. Tree house is a wish to have family goals met.**

COLORPLATE 113

The person unable to reach the lofty expectations of family is killed. Unfortunately, they were not even the person's own goals.

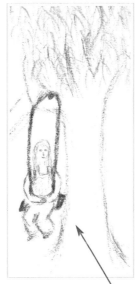

COLORPLATE 114

The person desires a break or vacation from seeking goals. *Note* she is looking forward.

COLORPLATE 115

The tire-swing provides the opportunity to relax. *Note* the apples (rewards) on ground. These are rewards or missed opportunities.

COLORPLATE 116

The person looking away is distracting herself along her path of life (day dreaming). *Note* the birds. See section on what birds represent, pg. 37.

Scene from "The Bad Seed," 1956. Thinking of ways to destroying lives?

COLORPLATE 117

Swinging while future explodes. *Note* the Richter scale grass measuring quake strength.

COLORPLATE 118

COLORPLATE 119

The person is contemplating her future, yet she is undecided on the course.

COLORPLATE 120

Future portends grimness, and the person is resigning himself to this (depressed).

COLORPLATE 121

The person is distracting himself from making a decision about his future. *Note* **the book has Psych. written on it.**

COLORPLATE 122

COLORPLATE 123

The person is the tree and is looking into the house for approval.

One way to counter the oppressive family is to react with rage. "Take this job and shove it." *Note* the **prominent garage and recessed door.**

Birds represent desire to escape from fenced-in life. *Note* the **faceless people, but defined dog and prominent garage.**

The birds are flying away from home, and the only escape is across the water. *Note* the **person without feet and bleak tree.**

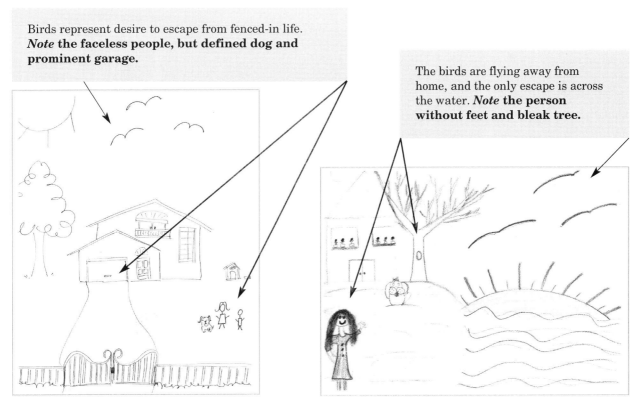

COLORPLATE 124

COLORPLATE 125

COLORPLATE **126**

Clouds represent depression in the person's life. *Note* **the windowless house and people with no eyes (see no evil).**

COLORPLATE **127**

Clouds and birds in a psychedelic scene. A person self-medicates in order to cope with her depression.

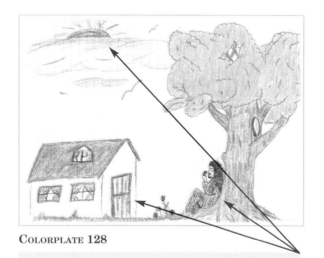

COLORPLATE **128**

Sun represents father's influence. *Note* **the clouds symbolizing depression. Door on side of house, person reclining against tree, taking time to smell the roses, all represent avoiding contact.**

COLORPLATE **129**

Sun obscured by clouds and rainbow, reflecting a manic/depressed approach to life in father. *Note* **the birds equal a desire to escape. Exposed branches in tree, windows into future, if one could only escape the house.**

COLORPLATE 130

Sun is over couple representing father's influence over relationship. *Note* **the door on side of house and red angry color, hole in the tree.**

COLORPLATE 131

Sun is over tree representing father's influence over future and goals. *Note* **the bleakness of the house structure and tree. Roof has a compartmentalized appearance; the person is conflicted, not wanting to upset people in the house.**

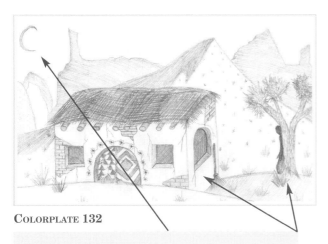

COLORPLATE 132

The moon represents the mother's influence on the present. *Note* **the dilapidated, primitive, empty structure, meeting few needs. The person is a shadowy colorplate behind the tree living in a stark landscape. The moon is waning.**

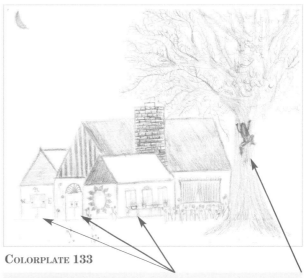

COLORPLATE 133

The moon is positioned over house as in Colorplate 132, influence of mother is strong beyond the house. *Note* **Again a shadowy colorplate this time pursuing goals as if secretly (stealthily). Appearance of three houses, the main one closed off and one looking for direction (compass).**

Note the sun and clouds.
Father is depressed.

Note the shuttered house
and explosive tree.

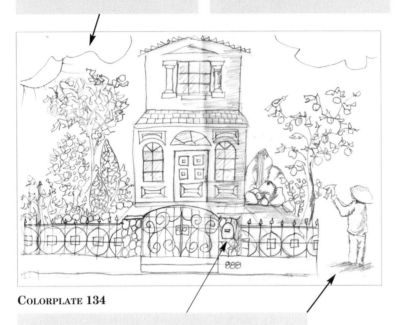

COLORPLATE 134

COLORPLATE 135

Mailboxes represent passively regarding future.
Note the faceless person without feet.

Person waiting for information that
is so urgent she will stand in the
road. The mail truck better have
good brakes.

chapter 6

Animals

Animals in the picture represent the need to be loved unconditionally. The artist that puts animals in the pictures has not received unconditional love in his or her life and thus invests this need into his or her pets (Figures 136–138). Unconditional love is defined as love that exists between two people regardless of the behavior of the people. Often caregivers are conditional in that affection is withdrawn when the offending person, usually a child, has done something wrong according to the caregiver. The caregiver personalizes the wrongdoing and labels the child as "bad" for having done what he or she has done. The parent's affection is then conditional on the child being good. People erroneously believe that pets are unconditional, that they are non-judgmental, completely accepting the owner, regardless of that owner's behavior. Animals do not have the capacity to be non-judgmental or judgmental. What makes the relationship between owner and pet unconditional is the capacity of the person. The owner is projecting his or her own goodness and ability to be unconditional on to the pet. If one observes animals, they are extremely conditional with each other. The fact that wolves and lions, which are not that far removed from our dogs and cats, tend to pick on the weak and sickly is evidence of conditional behavior. It is humans that say, "Pick on somebody your own size." That loving, caring dog will growl and bark at any innocent person who walks by its yard. That loving, caring cat will leave its owner when the neighbors have better food. Don't misunderstand; pets are wonderful and enrich people's lives, but it is people who put all their best qualities onto pets rather than the reverse (see pgs. 87–89, Self-Esteem Measure and Explanation).

Animals project a need for unconditional love. Person appears trapped in house with only cat for comfort. *Note* **house off the paper and stairs up to obscure door. Tree bleak, lifeless, as is the future.**

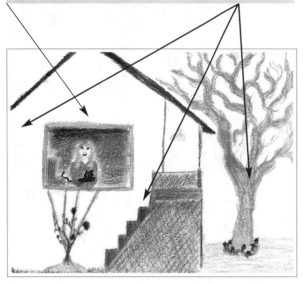

FIGURE 136

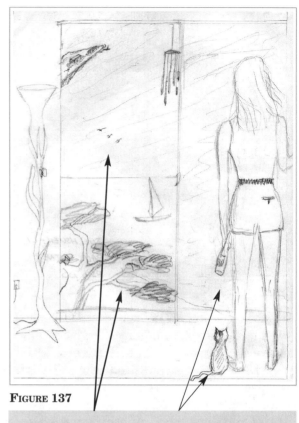

FIGURE 137

Person and her cat looking away at life that is passing by. *Note* **birds = desire for freedom, free is a bonsai representing a stunted, manipulated future.**

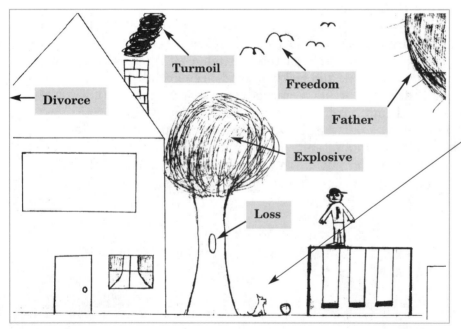

FIGURE 138

Divorce

Turmoil

Freedom

Father

Explosive

Loss

Male person with dog attending to him; he is balanced precariously on swing set. *Note* **the house off paper = divorce, smoke = turmoil, sun = father's influence outside of home, hole in tree = loss, tree = explosive future.**

chapter 7

Overall Schema

House lifeless

Unconscious violated

Dead future

Loss

FIGURE 139

Person withdrawn, collapsed with depression.

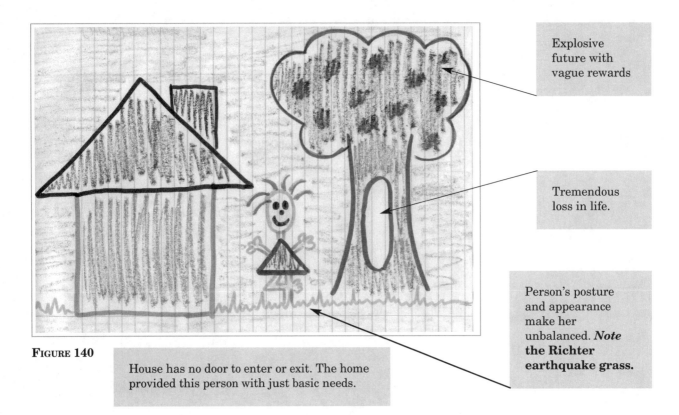

FIGURE 140

Explosive future with vague rewards

Tremendous loss in life.

Person's posture and appearance make her unbalanced. *Note* **the Richter earthquake grass.**

House has no door to enter or exit. The home provided this person with just basic needs.

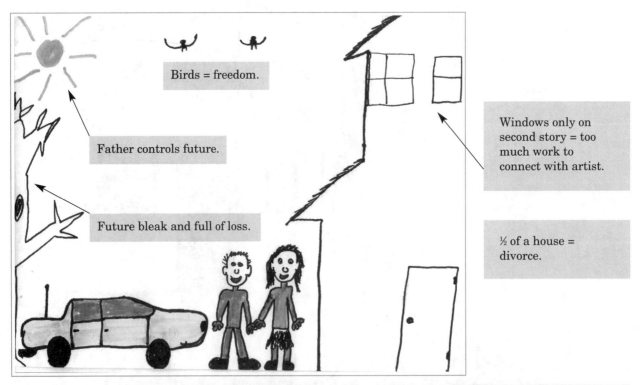

FIGURE 141

Birds = freedom.

Father controls future.

Future bleak and full of loss.

Windows only on second story = too much work to connect with artist.

½ of a house = divorce.

Car representing desire for freedom, escape, and this will be accomplished through a relationship formed outside of the home. Couple seems well connected despite a rather unfulfilling past. However, couple may only be connected in their mutual desire to run away.

FIGURE 142

Cloudy future. Depression is unlikely to lift soon.

There is an easier path to the future if the depression would subside; the path is represented by steps on the tree. Blue = sadness.

Scene is flooded with depression. The person appears trapped and looks as if he too is raining tears. Red (angry) door and overall scene contradict the welcome mat.

FIGURE 143

Faint clouds and birds

Slight perfectionism reflected in roof

Faint loss

Open connected person (hands and eye contact) reflecting rather open house. Windows are at door level. Tree has branches and leaves reflecting a positive picture for the future.

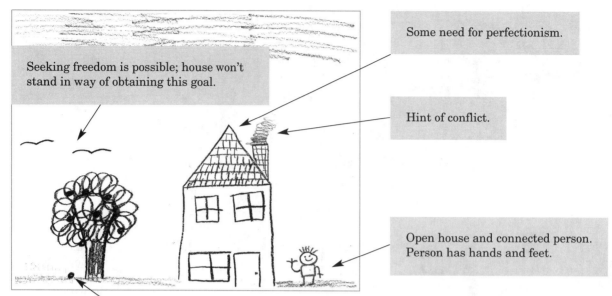

Seeking freedom is possible; house won't stand in way of obtaining this goal.

Some need for perfectionism.

Hint of conflict.

Open house and connected person. Person has hands and feet.

FIGURE 144

Future has rewards, but some paths are unclear. Fruit on ground represents obtained goal or missed opportunity, which may be freedom.

Roof and unconscious are transparent; what you see is what you get.

Family and goals tied together and guarded by fence. What the family expects of the person is unclear to the artist.

FIGURE 145

Relatively open house. Lower level windows obscured with curtains. Person reflects the closed quality with his hands withdrawn.

Birds = escape.

House appears open but structurally unsound.

Odd roofline; unconscious, overexposed, no boundaries.

Dead stump for future. What kind of future could a stick man have?

Self-identified as stick man.

FIGURE 146

chapter **8**

Drawings to be Analyzed

You analyze:
More to analyze on pgs. 131 and 132

FIGURE 147

FIGURE 148

FIGURE 149

chapter **9**

Index of Symbols

Animals = need for unconditional love

Bird = freedom, desire to break the bounds of the earth

Car = desire to obtain freedom

Chimney = phallic symbol, father's influence in the home

Clouds = sadness, depression

Curtains = obscuring family life, keeping people at a distance

Door = ability to enter and exit past

Eyes = ability to connect and engage with others, window to soul

Feet = ability to move from one's current place in life

Fence = need to be guarded, protected, trapped

Hands = ability to connect to others

Hole in tree = loss experienced in life

House = family, security, basic needs, reflection of past, mother's influence in home

Moon = mother's influence on the present

Mailbox = waiting for information about future

Nest = desire for family

Owl = wisdom gained from loss

Person = graphic representation of self

Rain = depression

Roofline = how much unconscious material the artist has, what he or she is unaware of

Shingles = perfectionism, obsessiveness, containment of unconscious impulses or desires

Smoke = turmoil, conflict in house, reflective presence of fire/anger

Squirrel = having gone "nuts" due to loss

Sun = father's influence on the present

Tree = goals, future, growth potential

Windows = openings into family and past

chapter 10

Additional Materials

These materials to provide you with a deeper understanding of your drawing will be found on the following pages:

Tests and checklist are provided for educational and informational purposes, not diagnostic.

Freud Primer

According to Freud, We Are All Somewhat Disturbed

FREUD CREATES A THEORY BASED ON SEXUAL AND AGGRESSIVE DRIVES

Freud wanted his theory of personality to be as scientific as possible. He wanted psychology to be elevated beyond a philosophy of human behavior to the scientific approach on a par with physics or chemistry. In order to do this, Freud concluded that he must root his theory in biology. He was strongly influenced by Darwin, whose theory implied survival of the fittest. The fittest are those biological creatures that find an environment and exploit it. A creature proved it was the fittest by reproducing, filling that void with more of that creature than other creatures. Freud asked how humans are different than any other creature. He concluded that humans were not different. Humans were driven by the same thing as every other biological creature: the drive to reproduce. Initially, according to Freud, a reproductive or sexual drive is behind all behavior.

Freud had some difficulty explaining all behavior as a sexual drive, so he concluded that there must be another drive, the aggressive drive. He believed that humans were hedonistic creatures, driven by pleasure, a desire to have all of one's needs met. He proposed that there are two states when all of our needs are met. One state is in the womb. The womb is the perfect environment, 98.6 degrees, not a care or want. People would like to go back to the womb, and they try to every night. They crawl into bed, pull up the covers, curl up in the fetal position, and recreate the perfect womb-like environment. But something goes wrong, a baby cries, a dog barks, someone rolls over in the bed, and the person wakes up. People can only symbolically go back to the womb, and thus people are inherently frustrated.

Not being able to return to the womb except symbolically, people try to obtain the other state in which all needs are met. This state is known as death. In death, there are no wants, desires, or cares. People want to go back to the womb, but they can't. However, people *can* obtain the other state. Freud called this second drive the aggressive drive, a drive based on a desire for death (self-destruction). Freud stated that all people have a "Death Wish." However, when people are dead, they cannot fulfill the other (sexual) drive. The two basic drives that underlie all behavior and thought, according to Freud, are therefore in conflict with each other. People want to sexually reproduce, and people want to be dead, but they can't do both, so the best anyone can get out of life is a compromise, a little satisfaction of one at the sacrifice of the other. Freud's theory is a very pessimistic one; people can't always get what they want no matter how hard they try.

SOCIALLY ACCEPTABLE EXPRESSION
OF THE SEXUAL AND AGGRESSIVE DRIVES

Freud suggested that these two basic drives must be satisfied in socially acceptable ways. The sexual or reproductive drive and the aggressive (self-destructive) drive must be expressed within social confines. Obviously, it is not socially acceptable to have uncontrolled sexual relationships or to kill one's self in any culture. If people engage in uncontrolled sexual relationships, they are labeled derogatorily, or in some cultures, put to death. If a person attempts to kill himself, he is considered crazy, or at least disturbed. The person will be put into a mental health facility against his will and observed for at least 48 hours. Since the direct expression of the aggressive drive is self-destruction, which is socially unacceptable, it must be redirected into some acceptable form of aggression, and the sexual drive must be redirected as well.

Humans are not as physically capable as most of the other creatures with whom they co-existed and evolved along with. They don't have sharp fangs, they don't run very fast, they don't have sharp claws, but they do have large brains. With these big brains, humans formed social groups that allowed them to compete with the stronger, faster, more ferocious creatures. If all humans were competing with one another on a basic instinctual level, they would fight over sexual partners until one superior human was determined, and then a saber-toothed tiger would come along and eat the winner. The whole species is then gone; this is survival of the fittest. Forming social groups in order to survive meant that the basic drives had to be held down and redirected into socially acceptable ways.

The drives couldn't remain on a conscious level if they were to be expressed in socially acceptable ways. In essence, people had to act for the greater good of society if they were going to survive. Being part of the social group increased the individual's survivability but meant sacrificing immediate gratification of the sexual and aggressive drives. However, people could not consciously suppress these drives. With the evolution of consciousness came self-awareness. With self-awareness came selfishness, which meant that the individual would be less willing to sacrifice his needs for that of the group. If the drives remained conscious, he would not make that sacrifice because he could not understand how the sacrifice benefited *him*. His conscious mind would be overwhelmed with the decisions to be made about this sacrifice, and the person would not be able to function. So, the primitive drives moved out of the realm of consciousness to allow humans to concentrate on surviving in a complex society. Therefore, all social behavior is an unconscious expression of either the sexual or aggressive drive.

One might wonder how the sexual and aggressive drives are expressed in modern society. The sexual drive is expressed through our work. For example, being an author allows for the socially acceptable expression of the author's sexual drive. He can express the sexual drive symbolically by implanting or impregnating the reader with the seed of knowledge. He takes the reader's brain and puts an idea into it that never existed before. That reader then tells two friends about this new idea, and those two friends tell two friends, and so on. In this way, the author has become intellectually immortal, and he has indirectly fulfilled his sexual drive.

A teacher also expresses his aggressive drive in a socially acceptable way. He fulfills his aggressive drive by giving tests and making people study outside of the class, intruding into their family life and leisure time. These are mean acts, but he does it in the name of helping them achieve something. He is expressing his aggressive drive, and if they fail, he is directly expressing the self-destructive aspects of that drive. If he is defined as a teacher and his students fail, then he is a failure. His students express their aggressive drive by not paying attention in class, not reading, not studying. These are all aggressive behaviors directed at the teacher and destructive behaviors directed toward themselves. Many students and people make declarations at the beginning of a semester or the turn of the new year: "This semester I will get all my work done on time" or "This year, I will get in shape . . . eat right . . . get a new job . . . get a new relationship. . . ." Then, at the end of the semester or new year, they are just as big a "mess" in their mind as they were previously. This is called self-destruction.

THE PERSONALITY STRUCTURES: ID, EGO, AND SUPEREGO

The sexual and aggressive drives are expressed through personality structures. The majority of these personality structures, like the drives, are unconscious; in other words, people are unaware of how the personality structures are interacting in order to direct their lives. The personality structures are the Id, the Ego, and the Superego. The expression and fulfillment of the sexual and aggressive drives occur through the interaction of these personality structures.

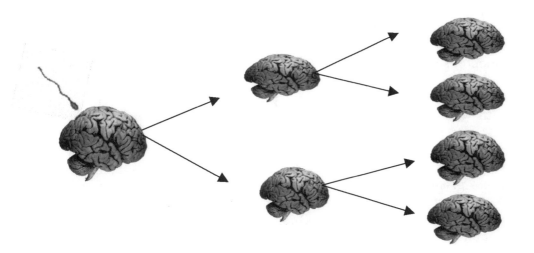

The Id

The first personality structure that we have is the Id. The Id contains and is directed by the sexual and aggressive drives. The Id translated from Latin means "it." We come into the world as an Id; it is the "me" part of us: "me" in the sense of not being concerned about others. The Id wants instant gratification. The Id operates on the Pleasure Principle, which involves fantasies about getting everything one desires and fulfilling those desires immediately. An infant has no concern about the rest of the world (it could be contended that the infant is not intellectually capable of being aware of its surroundings, but the Id is not intellectual; rather, it is emotional). If the infant needs something, it cries, not caring how tired its parents are, and that cry won't stop until the need is met. That cry is aggressive, it goes through walls, it goes through pillows, and it is unceasing. At first the infant is fed every time it cries, but eventually it is put on a feeding schedule. The Id does not appreciate this, but through this structure and delay, the Id realizes it can't go it alone. That crying all the time will be met with hostility or indifference, so the Id forms another personality structure to help it cope with a changing world. Out of the Id comes the Ego.

The Ego

The Ego's job is to satisfy the needs of the Id. The Ego is the "I" part of us; in Latin, Ego means "I." The Ego's duty is to get what "I" want for "Me." The Ego must delay gratification of the Id. The Ego is the thinking part; it uses different defenses to keep away anxiety (See pg. 83, list and explanation of defense mechanisms). The Ego operates on the Reality Principle, which dictates that people can't always get what they want. People can't cry all the time for the rest of their lives—bad things happen, and this is reality. In other words, life is generally unfair. The Ego has a difficult job trying to satisfy a greedy, needy beast. The Id's needs are never completely fulfilled by the nature of the two basic drives being in conflict with each other.

The Superego

The final personality structure to form is the Superego. Superego translates from Latin to mean "Above the I." The Superego is the moral part of us, the "They." What "They" say "I" can or can't do for "Me." The Superego's job is to punish the Ego and keep the Id's drives in check. The Superego has two parts: the Conscience and the Ego Ideal. The Conscience is the part of the Superego that allows for the individual to recognize what is wrong or inappropriate. The Ego Ideal is the part of the Superego that allows for the individual to recognize what is right or appropriate. These two parts of the Superego provide standards for appropriate and inappropriate behavior with which the person can judge his own behavior. These standards are based on a child's parents' Superego, on the parents' standard of what is morally right and wrong. The Superego was formed out of the Ego in order to keep the Id drives in check. All behavior, then, can be addressed as an Id, Ego, and Superego conflict: what is wanted for the "Me" part, what "I" think "I" can have, and what "They" say "I" should have. The poor Ego has the job of feeding this beast, the Id, while at the same time avoiding the punishment of the ideal standard of the Superego.

INTERACTION OF THE THREE PERSONALITY STRUCTURES

An example of an Id, Ego, and Superego conflict is when a student is sitting through what he perceives to be a boring lecture. The Id part of the student wants to go to sleep (self-destructive behavior in the classroom); the Ego part doesn't know what to do; and the Superego says, "Good students pay attention." So, the student ends up nodding off and waking up, and nodding off, and waking up. He gets neither a good sleep nor pays full attention, and this is the compromise the Ego strikes.

The Id is constantly generating desire while the Superego is countering those desires by generating guilt. Another example of the interactive process: someone suggests a person take a trip to a resort, and the Id says "Go now!" The Superego says, "What is wrong with you? You have work to do," and the Ego asks "What do I do?" The Id says, "Go now. Who cares about responsibilities?" The Superego counters, "Good students stay home and study, good employees do their work." Finally, the Ego reaches a compromise, and the person takes his books/work to the resort. The work is the last thing the person puts in the car and the last thing he takes out. Every time he sees his backpack or briefcase, he feels guilty and thinks "Oh, I should be doing that." This decision to bring the books/work compromises his enjoyment; his experience at the resort was not completely unrestricted fun. He felt guilty because he didn't do what he was supposed to do.

The Psychosexual Stages

These personality structures are formed in stages, and these are known as psychosexual stages, and what occurs during these stages is not part of one's consciousness, since the stages take place at such a young age. Each of these stages allows for different expressions of the sexual and aggressive drives. At different ages, different stages of development occur, and what occurs during these stages will result in the formation of the personality. These early childhood stages establish the foundation of the adult personality. The ideal message one needs to receive during these stages is that life is *generally* unfair and that the best one ever gets out of life is a compromise. If one were to receive the message that life is "fair" or that life is "totally unfair" specifically for that person, he will end up with a disturbed personality.

Limited Energy and Fixation

Freud proposed that humans are closed energy systems, that they have only so much energy. People talk about having only so much energy. They

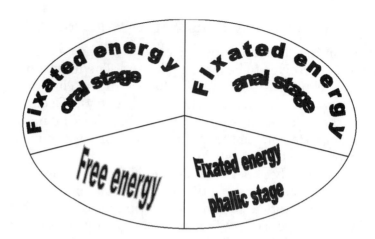

are trying to find balance between how much energy they put into their jobs, relationships, school, and home. Once they reach adulthood, people start to get sick and tired, mentally generating illness and weakness (see pg. 102, Stress Test Explanation). Young children will never admit sickness or tiredness until they are introduced to school, and then they are more than happy to admit they are sick. There are times when adults push the energy envelope, as in a woman giving birth. The woman during labor exceeds her normal limits of pain and endurance, but once the joyous event is over, she returns to her normal level of endurance.

Freud proposed that if some of this energy is stuck at one of the psychosexual stages, the person will have less energy to invest in later stages. Not only will he have less energy, he will continually make attempts to free this energy. The energy will be stuck, and he will only be able to symbolically try to free this energy. Freud's term for stuck or trapped energy is Fixation. Fixated energy can be released only by going back to the psychosexual stage where the energy became fixated and redoing what went wrong. For normal development of the personality, people need to receive the proper message about the realities of the world. The child needs to receive the message at each psychosexual stage that life is "unfair," and to receive any other message will result in the development of a disturbed personality. The child cannot receive a message that life is "fair" or "totally unfair" for him and develop a fully functioning personality because these messages result in fixation. If a person is overindulged—life is fair—he will fixate some energy. If the person is underindulged—life is totally unfair (specifically for him)—he will fixate some energy. The over and underindulged will have less energy for the next stage and subsequent stages. Depending on how early the wrong message occurred, nearly all of his energy could be fixated. If the foundation of a house is not properly laid, the whole house up to the roof will need to be repaired, but any repairs done *other than to the foundation* will be ineffective. The *only* repair that will be effective is to change the message to "unfair" from "fair" or "totally unfair." Replaying that stage is accomplished through the reinterpretation of how his parents treated him and can be done only with the help of a therapist. A person cannot repair himself because the interactions that caused the problem created an unconscious barrier to insight as to what the real problem or issue may be. Essentially, the person can't handle the truth, so he will deny his reality (see pg. 83, Defense Mechanisms).

ORAL STAGE

The first stage of the psychosocial stages is the Oral stage, and it encompasses ages birth-1. The expression and satisfaction of the two drives, sexual (reproductive drive) and aggressive (self-destructive drive), occur through the oral area of the body. The infant gets its needs met by crying and drinking from the bottle or the breast, and this is how the child perpetuates himself. Once an infant can crawl, he can explore the world, and when he comes in contact with an object, he puts it in his mouth, consuming the world (see pg. 22, Hands). How the parents meet these oral needs will be reflected in different personality types.

Orally-Dependent Personality

If the parents are overly attentive (too nice) to the needs of the child, the child does not have to work at all, and the child will have been overindulged and fixates (sticks) some energy at this stage. Life is "too fair," and the Id of the child wants to stay at this age forever. The parents have baby monitors and listen for any peep or cry and race into the baby's room to satisfy his every need. The parents reason that life is cruel enough and he will have a lifetime of work ahead of him, and if they can make this time worry- and work-free, then they will. The Id, living in a fantasy world, believes it can live there, but the Ego, which deals with reality, knows it can't. As the child grows older and life presents him with unfairness, the child and later adult will try going back to the time when things were good, but he can only do it symbolically, so he sucks his thumb. He is an orally-dependent person, and orally-dependent people as children suck or chew on things beyond the average age. As adults in times of stress, they smoke, drink, eat, talk too much, chew gum. Any time a person takes something outside of him and puts it into him to make himself feel a certain way because he cannot generate these feelings for himself is orally-dependent behavior. The orally dependent person, when there is not enough love in his world, fills in the void with chocolate cake or cigarettes. The heroin addict and the alcoholic look around their world and become depressed. To relieve this stress, the addict takes a needle (symbolically a baby bottle) and sticks it in the vein, and the alcoholic literally takes the bottle to make himself feel better (see pg. 14, Variation on Houses). In times of stress, orally-dependent people talk and talk about what worries them but delay doing anything about confronting the concern because this would end the talking. Chewing gum only makes some logical sense as long as there is flavor, but beyond that it's just an activity that stimulates and soothes the oral area of the body. Adults with "Binkies" or pacifiers in their mouths are not socially acceptable, but gum is. When do people smoke the most? When they are stressed or are overindulging themselves. The miniature baby bottle that soothes is being put into their mouth.

Orally-Aggressive Personality

If the parents are not attentive (too mean) to the needs of the child, the child has to work too hard, and the child will have been underindulged and fixates (sticks) some energy at this stage. Life is "unfair specifically" for this child, and the Id will express its aggression in relationships forever. The infant has to cry and cry and cry to get her needs met, and when the needs are finally attended to, it is in a very unsatisfactory way. The baby gets a cold bottle of formula. The baby wanted a nice warm breast or at least warm formula; the baby draws on the cold bottle and the Id says "This is unfair, and I won't forget this." The Id has been unsatisfied in its initial relationship, and as a child and later as an adult, the Id will recreate this disappointment and act aggressively in relationships. The child/adult will develop an orally-aggressive personality. Orally-aggressive people say mean things, and they say the meanest things to people they also say they love. People don't act as though they have Tourettes syndrome (Tourettes syndrome is a neurological disorder that causes sufferers to blurt out socially unacceptable words), saying mean things and swearing at strangers. All in the name of love, people say horrible things to people they care about. What they are doing is trying to destroy that person with their words, coming out of the oral area of their body. People say the meanest things not at the beginning of a relationship but at the end. As soon as the relationship becomes stressful, then the negative, degrading, disrespectful comments start. The orally-aggressive person is biting and tearing at his or her partner's sense of self. The orally-aggressive person goes into all relationships with the expectation that he or she is going to be disappointed and will naturally gravitate to people who will disappoint (see pg. 87, Self-Esteem Measure/Explanation). An orally-aggressive person makes generalizations about the other person in the relationship such as: "You always . . ." or "You never . . ."; choosing only to notice the times when he or she was disappointed.

Sarcasm and cynicism are other forms of orally-aggressive behavior. Sarcasm is mean, biting humor. Cynicism is a self-destructive, "the cup is half empty," approach to life. The person experiencing sarcasm mimics what the orally-aggressive person experienced as an infant. The infant wishes life would be fair, that everything would be all right if he or she did his or her job, which was to cry, but then crying wasn't enough; so as a result, he or she gets the unsatisfying bottle. With sarcasm, the orally-aggressive person sets up conditions so that the other person believes everything will turn out all right, but the sarcastic person ends up giving a verbal kick in the rear. An example: a person asks another person if he likes what the other person is wearing. The other person says "Yeah, it looks great!" (Everything is good.) "NOT!" (Everything turns bad.) Another common sarcastic comment which follows a person explaining himself to another is the word "Whatever." This comment is particularly aggressive in that the person usually makes eye contact (see pg. 21, Eyes) and appears to be listening to the person who is explaining himself just before the sarcastic person delivers the word "Whatever." Again the early experiences of the orally-aggressive person are being recreated, everything is seemingly all right, the person is being attended to, and then he is dismissed as not worthy of consideration, "Whatever." The ripped off end up ripping off.

Ego Structure Developed

By the end of the Oral stage, the child has developed a significant Ego structure. A child comes into this stage as an Id, but he is put on a feeding schedule, involving delay (Ego) and frustration. Then, as the child ages, he is further frustrated by being asked to produce language. At first the infant must merely cry to be fed, but then it is asked to specify what it wants "Binky or Baba?" The Id wants to scream and immediately be fed, but the Ego realizes it must figure out the right word or the Id may end up with nothing. Eventually, the Id is further frustrated because greater and finer distinctions of language are asked for: "Milk or Juice?" The Id would like to grab the drink it wants and throw the other at the parent, but the Ego waits and figures out the right word. Often people will go to a restaurant and look at all the choices on the menu and become overwhelmed, either rejecting all items as unappealing (aggression) or being desirous (sexual) of all the items. They then ask whoever they are with or the waiter or waitress to make the choice for them by asking, "What are you going to have?" or "What would you recommend?" This is the equivalent behavior of a child crying, "Mommy, feed me." Adults who believe they are in love will also feed each other bits of their meals while calling each other infantile names. An Id dream would be the person who was experiencing a lot of stress could go into a bar and just start crying and the bartender would immediately serve a drink to him or her rather than the person having to choose from a vast array of available drinks. At least the person could avoid some of the Id frustration by being able to point and say "Baba" or "Baba Lite."

The Anal Stage

The second psychosexual stage is the Anal stage. At the start of the Oral stage, the child is pure Id, and at the end, he should have significant Ego structure, due to frustration of feeding schedules and language development and the need to cope with that frustration. The Anal stage is when the Ego finishes the rest of its development. The Anal stage is when the child learns lessons about satisfaction and delay of that satisfaction regarding the sexual and aggressive drive in the anal area of the body. The age the child is in the Anal stage is from the 1-3 years, and the great task of this time is toilet training or "potty" training. Toilet training is the most complex learning a person goes through. A person may believe he has difficulty with the subject of algebra or English, but these are nothing compared to the learning that must occur during the Anal stage. The Anal stage is the first time in a child's life that he has to pay attention to how he physically feels. Previously, if the child had to go to relieve himself, he just did. If the child was hungry, he cried; too hot, he cried; too cold, he cried. There was no conscious (Ego) need to pay attention to internal feeling states. Then suddenly, a demand is made of the child to not only pay attention to how he feels but to do something about it. When he feels like he has to go to the bathroom, he has to get up and get himself over to this cold porcelain thing and sit on it.

A person often tries to express his or her feelings to another person and finds himself or herself misunderstood. The other person responds, "I don't know what you are saying" or "I don't know how you could feel that way," so now the person is not only being told he or she is not understood but also how he or she should feel. In the Anal stage, the child is being told "Hey you. When you feel this way, do something about it," yet that child never had to pay attention to feelings before. That is very complex learning. Before, the child's feeling states may have been commented on, but there was never any consequence. The child cries and an adult may say, "Oh, you are sad," or the child smiles and an adult may say "Oh, you are happy," but the labeling of sadness or happiness has no meaning to the child. There is not a sudden demand made to be happier or sadder. However, in the Anal stage, an immediate demand is made on the child to change his feeling state, to relieve himself in the right place at the right time. If the child doesn't go about his "business" in the right manner, there can be serious consequences and comments made about the child's ability to control himself.

The first artistic thing a child makes might be a collage, a hand print in clay, a drawing, or a painting. This piece of art is often made as a gift and given to the child's parents. Actually, the first thing a child ever makes for his or her parents was his or her bowel movement. How they responded to that gift will reflect upon that person and everything else he makes of himself. If those initial gifts (bowel movements) are accepted, then so will anything else the child makes. If they and the child are rejected, so will all other creations.

Anally-Retentive Personality

I recall witnessing a child's diaper being changed; the child was 6 months old. The work of a 6-month-old is to eat, to sleep, and to move her bowels. The mother of this child opened the diaper and said, "Oh Jesus, you stink." This child's gift was rejected, not only the gift but the child herself. A third of this child's existence is going to the bathroom (the other two-thirds are eating and sleeping), and she "stinks" at it. Not only does she "stink" at it, but the mother must evoke the name of the Lord to help her cope with it. This seems like an innocuous comment in the life of a 6-month-old. After all, how much will she remember, and it probably occurs thousands of times a day with mothers and fathers all over the world in different languages. However, this is only the start of the rejection of gifts because almost everything that directs the child's and adult's life is unconscious, and what occurs at 6 months will reoccur at six years and 60 years and all the years in between. A very different message would be presented to the child if when the diaper was opened the mother declared, "Wow, what a great poop! You are doing such a good job! Now we have to clean this poop up." The child and the excrement are separated; the child is doing its work and doesn't "stink" at it. Remember, these stages affect the development of the child's adult personality, but what occurs at each stage is a reflection of the parents' personality. Since the processes that govern people's personalities are unconscious, the mother or father has no idea how or why he or she is rejecting the gifts, and that is why most people consider their drawings and drawing abilities as inadequate. Moving the time line along, the child with the dirty diaper is now three years old and presents a drawing she has

made to the mother. The mother will see it and respond, "Honey, what is it?" The child responds, "It is a doggy." The mother then starts critiquing the "doggy," cleaning it up so it looks more like what the mother thinks a doggy should look like. The parent, who similarly can only make inadequate drawings, can only fix it so much and ends the art lesson in frustration saying "Well, that is the best I can do."

The diaper stinks, necessitating clean up, the drawing stinks, necessitating clean up, and both gifts are rejected. The child, later the adult, can no longer cope with stress brought on by expressing or distracting herself by drawing. If she tries to draw, this only leads to further frustration. Because of the critical nature of the child's training at this age, he is cut off from the artistic form of self-expression. This book has attempted to illustrate how deeply significant drawing can be for self-expression, a means of expression that is so often terminated at an early age. In response to stress, the person who had a punitive "unfair" Anal stage often regresses back to Oral stage behaviors, such as orally-aggressive behavior (sarcasm and cynicism) or orally-dependent behavior (drinking and smoking). The child is now six years old and brings home the report card from school with two smiley faces and one frown. The parent doesn't erupt in joy emphasizing the smiley faces and make comments that the child is so smart and doing a good job. Rather, the parent looks at the frowning face and says, "What the hell is this? No kid of mine is this dumb. This is unacceptable. Your brother did better than this." The child is now 16 and brings home someone who is significant to her. The parent doesn't embrace the person and welcome him into the home. Rather, the parent sneers in disapproval and says, "Don't bring that S_ _ _ around here. You can do better than that." In response, the child who is now showing many of the characteristics of the parent replies, "Oh yeah? Did you, Mom?"

The parent sees toys all over the floor and says, "What is all this crap on the floor?" Actually, those are cars, and those are blocks, and those are stuffed animals. The parent is wearing fecal-matter-colored glasses, identifying all objects not in their place as bowel movements. Unconsciously, the parent has a need to degrade and destroy everything he or she sees. The parents who are "too mean" and overly critical of the child's ability to control her bowel movement and ultimately make something of herself create an anally-retentive person.

Anally-retentive people constantly clean; they are concerned about making a mess, or doing something shameful (see pg. 10, Shingles). Many people clean when they are experiencing stress. The rest of their life might be spinning out of control, but at least their oven, house, and car are clean.

Anally-retentive people will also collect items. Symbolically, they are collecting all those bowel movements that they had to get rid of before they

were ready. It is not socially acceptable to collect bowel movements, but it is to collect Beanie Babies, shoes, hats, money, cars, and baseball cards. The "totally unfair" message has resulted in a fixation of energy at the Anal stage. Collecting is related to the child's sense of having lost part of himself down the toilet. One has to remember that at the age at which toilet training is occurring, the child is only capable of using a child's thought processes of that age; the thought processes are on a limited logical level, consisting of statements such as "You are what you eat." The bowel movement is just an extension of the child. Literally, that is a bit of the child going down the toilet, and he acknowledges it. If one observes a child during this age, he will go to the bathroom and then look in the bowl and say "That one looks like a baby duck, and that one looks like a mommy duck," flushing the toilet he will then say "Bye."

Anal-Expulsive Personality

What if the parents are "too nice" and avoid punishment and shame around toilet training, allowing the child to develop in her own time with regard to toilet training? The parents do not impose control and Ego structure on the child, and this will also result in a fixation, life is "fair." The child and later the adult will develop an anally-expulsive personality. To be expulsive means to throw outward. Anally-expulsive people are messy. They have messy rooms, messy lives, and messy relationships. Any behavior that goes against logic (Ego) is emotionally driven (Id). It makes the most logical sense that when people are stressed due to demands and deadlines, they should organize. If people become more disorganized as the stress levels increase, they are acting irrationally and are anally expulsive. Many people have anally-expulsive relationships: the relationship doesn't have a clean ending, and it is messy, so flush "Bye." People rarely end relationships without getting angry and spilling their anger all over each other. The relationship ends and both people hang on to feelings. They degrade (mess) the other person they at one time loved. People often get into relationships that they intellectually know are not right for them, so they break up. One or both parties continue to think (obsess) about the other after the break up and end up getting back together, only to find out again the relationship doesn't work. There is not a clean end to this chapter of life. Many anally-expulsive people are haunted by memories of past relationships and loves lost. Anally-expulsive people are so enmeshed in their relationships that they put anger and stress onto their family, rather than direct it at the true source. They rely too heavily on the Ego defense of displacement (see pg. 83, Defense Mechanisms).

By the end of the anal stage, the person has nearly a completely formed Ego structure and most of its defense mechanisms to cope with anxiety. The only personality not formed yet is the Superego.

THE PHALLIC STAGE

The third psychosexual stage is the phallic stage, and it encompasses the ages of 3-5. A phallic symbol is anything that resembles the male genitals. The idea behind this stage is that this is the age at which children start to notice anatomical differences between males and females. Again using the children's thought process of this age, they are trying to reason what accounts for these differences. In the logic of the child, what anatomical parts are on one person and not on another must have fallen off or have been chopped off. Children don't know that fetuses are anatomically female until 6 weeks old and genetically determined to be male. Freud proposed that at this age (3–5 years), all male children go through what is called the Oedipal Complex. Freud looked to various cultures to find universal stories about human personality development. In the Greek tragedy *Oedipus Rex*, he found a story that explained the experiences of all male children.

Briefly, the story of *Oedipus Rex* is that of a queen who had a dream. The queen's dream, like all dreams, was confusing. So, the queen went to her court dream interpreter to find out the dream's meaning. Freud wrote that dreams were the royal road to the unconscious (*The Interpretation of Dreams,* 1900). The interpreter said the dream meant that the queen was going to have a child, and that child would be a boy. That boy would end up killing the king, her husband, and end up marrying her, the queen. The queen was horrified by the dream and had the messenger, the interpreter, killed. The queen gave birth to a son, the first part of the prophesy, and called upon another member of her court. She told this member of the court to get rid of the baby. The member of the court could not see his way to do this, so he put the baby in a basket and placed it in the river. The basket floated down the river. A fisherman found it and brought it ashore. He took the baby home and raised him as his own. The baby grew up to become a strapping knight who wanted to seek his fortune. Traveling the path of life, the knight ran into an old knight who blocked his way, and the young knight said, "Step aside, old man. I don't wish to kill you. You are old, I am young, and your time has passed." The old knight taunted the young knight and refused to move. The two came to blows, and the young knight ended up killing the old. The knight continued on his path of life and met a queen who just so happened to have recently lost her husband. The two fell in love. It turns out Oedipus had killed his father and married his mother.

Freud said this is not just a fable but an unfolding of events in all male children's lives. A boy would like to have the mother, his primary love object, to himself and eliminate the father. After all, it is the mother who feeds and diapers the baby. Even one hundred years past Freud's writing of his theory, mothers take care of 80% of all childcare in the Western world. What does the father do for the male child? He takes away the affections of the mother and hands out punishment ("Wait till your father gets home.").

The male child just wishes dad would go away so he could have mom to himself. The Id says to the child "Yes, get rid of dad," but the Ego says "I don't know." Then the Ego comes to a shocking revelation: if dad finds out about my plan, he might say, "Oh, you want your mommy to yourself. How about I make you like a little mommy?" Chop! Freud proposed that all male children at this age develop castration anxiety, that if the father finds out about the grand plan, he will make the male child into a female.

The father does not have to create a fear of literal castration; he can evoke verbal castration. The father can make comments about the child being a "Mama's boy" or "Crying like a girl." The anxiety builds and builds in the child to the point of unbearable proportions. The Id has no problem with the chopping. It says "Why stop there? Chop me all up." The Ego points out if we are chopped to pieces, we might be dead, satisfying the aggressive drive, but we won't be able to satisfy the sexual drive. The Ego comes to a compromise, Mom likes Dad, Dad likes Mom, for at least the two minutes necessary for conception. If "I" act like a little Dad, Mom will like me, Dad will like me, and my penis will not get chopped off. Eliminating the castration anxiety and resolving the Oedipal Complex, the Ego has compromised, and the male child now identifies with the same sex parent, in this case his father. By identifying with the father, the boy takes on all the morals of the father and now has a functioning Superego.

Essentially, Freud's theory says that by age 5, having gone through all the stages, one's personality is completely formed, and everything one does from then on is just a matter of going back and dealing with something that happened between birth and 5 years of age. Errors in Superego development can occur in a number of ways. If the father is an amoral person who is acting aggressively with the son, then the castration anxiety is very real. The male child develops tremendous fear that if the father finds out about this scheme to get Mother to himself, he will really inflict damage; after all, he is doing so with no reason already. There is great pressure to resolve the Oedipal Complex and identify with the father and take on his morals. But, there is a problem: the father has no morals, so the child ends up with a weak Superego which can't keep his aggressive drive in check. The boy ends up acting out the same way as the father, getting in fights and hurting others. He has no "Thou shalt nots" on his moral compass. A child can also have a father in his life that has an overly punitive Superego which does not allow for any pleasure. The child feels guilty any time he does something fun and must justify all pleasure in his life.

Females go through a similar crisis known as the Electra Complex. This story, too, is a Greek tragedy, and in it the girl is the protagonist. At the end of the story she ends up with her father having eliminated her mother. The mother, like the father in the Oedipal Complex, doesn't have to literally instill a fear of castration but can do so in more symbolic ways, such as referring to her as a "Daddy's girl" or "tomboy" and cutting her hair. There is a problem with applying this story to Freud's system of Superego development. Females have nothing to chop off. So, Freud proposed that since females have nothing to chop off, they have less castration anxiety and less pressure to identify with the same sex parent, in this case the mother. Since there is less pressure to identify with the mother, resolution of the Electra Complex results in weaker Superego. Thus, according to

Freud, women are less moral than men, and are dependent on men for moral guidance. Not only are women less moral, but they suffer from penis envy and are sexually inadequate without fulfillment of the man.

Reading about Freud's theory is understandable and relatable to many with regard to the drives, the personality structures, and even the first two stages, but the phallic stage tends to stretch the imagination of most. The following are some examples of children going through the Oedipal Complex. One child I worked with was four years old and a tremendous athlete. At this age, he was able to hit a baseball thrown overhand at a rapid speed. This boy and a number of other children, along with therapists in a group therapy program, were playing baseball, engaging in play therapy. The boy was left handed and was hitting with a hard plastic bat. I was throwing a tennis ball, and a female therapist was standing on first base. I threw the ball, and the boy hit a line drive up the first base line and right into the female therapist's groin. The amount of time it took the ball to leave the bat and hit the therapist was at best one half a second. As soon as it hit, the boy yelled, "Knocked it off!" The concern about having things "Knocked off" must be just barely under the surface to be spoken of so quickly.

To give a little history of this boy, his parents were getting divorced because the father had had an affair with the mother's best friend, and the only time the boy saw his father was when he took him to baseball practice. The boy, who drew the picture of the smoky house on pg. 12, came to group therapy one day declaring he had a dream. The dream was about being in a cabin, and a person in a hockey mask came into the cabin carrying a chain saw. The person in the mask started chasing the boy, and as he chased the boy, he was cutting up the furniture. The boy ran through the cabin to his mother, and just as he was about to get to his mother, he felt the blade of the chainsaw cutting into his neck, starting to cut off his head. He woke up. A very castration anxiety-driven dream, and Freud wrote "Dreams are the royal road to the unconscious" (*The Interpretation of Dreams*, 1900).

After the boy told this dream, the group was engaging in an art therapy activity. The children were to make kites and put wishes on the tails of the kites and then fly them into the air. The first wish the boy had me write was "I love my mother," the next was "I want to marry my mother." Freud got up out of his grave, clapped his hands, and fell back in.

Defense Mechanisms

The following is a list of defense mechanisms used by the Ego to protect the person from anxiety. All these defense mechanisms are necessary for emotional stability. People become emotionally unstable when they rely too heavily on one defense exclusively.

Compensation The emphasis of new goals or characteristics because the original goal or characteristic cannot be achieved or expressed. Example: A person excels in athletics because academically he is weak; or a short person becomes an actor and becomes larger than life on the movie screen.

Denial The rejection of stimuli that are threatening to the person. The person fails to acknowledge that a threat exists. Example: A refusal to perceive characteristics in oneself that others point out, such as a lack of control over drinking behavior or anger.

Displacement The channeling of drives or feelings toward a safer or more tolerant source than toward those who initially aroused the drive or feeling. Example: Yelling at the children because one is frustrated with one's spouse or work situation.

Projection The attributing of one's characteristics and motives to other or all people. Example: A dishonest person proclaiming that everyone is dishonest; or an angry person accusing another of being angry all the time.

Rationalization The justification of aggressive or unacceptable behavior in acceptable terms or reasons. Example: A person saying something hurtful and claiming he was "just teasing"; or someone explaining that he is chronically late because of traffic.

Regression The reaction to threatening or frustrating situations in a way that is more consistent to an early age or level of development. Example: The adult yelling and throwing things during an argument in the manner of a 2-year-old having a temper-tantrum; the adult drinking alcohol to soothe his feelings in the manner of an infant with a bottle.

Reaction Formation The act of responding to threatening or overwhelming situations or people with the opposite behavior than would be appropriate to one's feelings. Example: A person thanking a police officer for giving him a ticket when he is actually seething inside.

Repression The exclusion of thoughts, feelings, and desires from consciousness, making them unconscious. Example: Not being able to recall traumatic events and the feelings associated with the event, or failing to remember times when family members disappointed or embarrassed the person.

Sublimation The directing of unacceptable impulses into socially acceptable behaviors or goals. Example: The person with violent or destructive drives becoming a police officer or soldier; the surgeon who cuts people open and removes organs in the name of helping people.

Concept of Self-Esteem

This is a measure of self-esteem. A score of 12 and above implies average to good self-esteem. A score of 12 and below implies average to poor self-esteem. Self-esteem is an assessment of whether a person likes himself or herself and is confident in who he or she is. Questions arise if one scored in the poor range: what can one do about it? Looking at the items that are on the measure, many have to do with family: "My family pushes me too hard," etc. The idea behind this is the family environment is where one's sense of self develops.

If the family is unconditional in its love and attention, a strong sense of self will develop. Unconditional love means that regardless of behavior, the family will always love the child and not label him or her negatively. In other words, the behavior of the child is separated from the liking of the child. Unconditional example: The child doesn't pick up his or her toys; the parent does not immediately label that child as "Bad" and send him to his room, physically expressing a desire not to have the child present. The parent gives consequences with regard to the behavior separate from the child. A Conditional example: The child doesn't pick up his or her toys; the parent immediately labels that child as "Bad" and sends him to his room after swatting him on the rear end. Over time, negative messages from the family become incorporated into the sense of self, and we start acting in ways reflecting this poor sense of self. We end up putting ourselves in environments that reinforce our poor sense of self and avoiding ones that don't match this self-image (see pg. 21, Eyes). People tend to behave in a manner that reflects their self-image: "Bad people" do bad things, and "Good people" do good things.

As I was working as a consultant to an elementary school providing therapy to children who were deemed "at-risk," I noticed two things. One was that all the children who were identified as "at-risk" were from different classes at a very large school, but they all knew and played with one another. I realized this is how gangs are formed: all the "bad kids" hang out together, and they share experiences and self-images. The second thing I learned was that even in institutions that should know better, little is understood about the concept of self-esteem. The children who were supposed to receive the treatment were children who were "at-risk." "At-risk" was defined as children with self-esteem issues that might lead them to later engage in alcohol and tobacco consumption. The children who were referred to me were children who had experienced significant life traumas that affected them beyond just their self-esteem. All the children were in the third grade and approximately 8 years old: One's father recently had died in a car accident, one's parents were schizophrenic and manic depressed, and one had been molested. Two of the children later ended up being hospitalized. What I was dealing with were not children who needed help with their self-esteem, but rather children with issues of security (see pg. 5, Doors).

There is a theory that people have different levels of needs, all requiring satisfaction. At the lowest level are basic survival needs, such as food, water, and air. The next level is safety and security needs, then attention or love needs, and finally self-esteem needs. These children were dealing with the security level and/or the love level, both of which are levels below self-esteem (see illustration below). Yet, they were referred to the self-esteem group by teachers who were trained in what type of child would be appropriate to the group. The children were referred, even though they were inappropriate for the program, because the teachers were unable to properly provide for these disturbed children in a regular classroom. The school districts no longer have the financial means to provide appropriate placement for these children. Anytime these children were out of the classroom, the classroom was more functional.

A specific incident with one of these children will illustrate the difference between the security level and the self-esteem level. I went to pick up one of the children from his classroom, and upon entering the room, I noticed that the class was working on math problems the teacher was writing on the board. I inquired as to where the child I was to see was and was directed to the coat closet. I could hear grunts, moans, and the crashing of lunch pails coming from the closet. I went to the closet and found the boy under a number of coats and lunches. I asked what he was doing and he said "Looking for my snack." We left to go to the playground to talk and let him eat his snack. When we sat down, he took a sandwich out of the lunch bag, took a bite, and declared "This is my mother." He then proceeded to drop the sandwich on the ground, step on it, and grind it into the blacktop. If I were to try to help this boy with his self-esteem issues, many levels above where he is need-wise, I would make a comment such as, "Wow, you are the craziest, nuttiest boy I have ever met, isn't that great," for that comment would be dealing with self-esteem issues. Rather, I said "You seem to be really mad at your mother," and I watched him take out a cookie, declare it was his father, and smash it on the ground. This boy needed much more help than any self-esteem building session could provide; he needed a new family, something I was not in a position to provide. I was not going to keep this child from using tobacco or alcohol with a self-esteem group; he needed intense therapy to keep him out of a hospital.

The theory of need level proposes that a person cannot even begin to try to satisfy a higher need until all the lower needs have been satisfied. Unless the boy referred to above gets his safety and love needs attended to, his self-esteem issues cannot be addressed. Often people will attempt to meet higher needs with lower needs because the lower needs are available or abundant. For example, there is not a lot of love in a person's world, but there is plenty of snack food; or a person will get into a relationship that is secure but provides little or no love.

Referring back to the Self-Esteem measure, item #15 spells it out: "I have a low opinion of myself," or #3 "There are lots of things about myself I'd change if I could." There are not too many more damning statements than these with regard to one's sense of self. This brings us to the second question, "What can we do about changing this negative sense of self?" If one is to change his or her sense of self, he or she has to stress himself or herself, put himself or herself in environments that are uncomfortable. The more secure a person becomes with himself or herself, the less outside influences will affect his or her feelings. The quickest way to change one's self-image is to change one's environment. If a family, a relationship, or a workplace is damaging one's image, one has a self-obligation to get out of it or at least develop a plan with steps on how and when one will be free of the self-destructive place.

This is an illustration titled *The Two Towers* by a 7-year-old. The self-esteem of children is more volatile than that of adults, since their sense of self is less defined. Children can feel happy and competent in their abilities one moment, sad and diminished the next, depending on what is happening in their immediate environment.

Narcissism Checklist Key

1	B ✓		21	B ✓	
2	B		22	A ✓	
3	A ✓		23	B	
4	A		24	B	
5	A		25	B ✓	
6	A		26	B	
7	B		27	B	
8	B		28	A	
9	A		29	B ✓	
10	A		30	A	
11	A		31	A ✓	
12	B		32	A	
13	B		33	B	
14	A		34	B	
15	B ✓		35	B	
16	B		36	A ✓	
17	A		37	A	
18	A ✓		38	B ✓	
19	A		39	A	
20	A ✓		40	A	

12

Concept of Narcissism

The responses that match your response are worth one point. Total all matches and this is your Narcissistic score. Scores normally are 20 and below (Scores below 10 may reflect low self-image). Narcissism is different from self-esteem; it is self-absorption rather than self-love. Briefly, the story of Narcissus is he was walking along, saw a pond, looked down and saw his reflection, and fell in love with it. The concept of how much self-love one should have, and when it crosses the line into narcissism, is unclear. People are raised to believe that they are to have a healthy sense of self, but an excessive self-image is considered conceited. In essence, we are socialized to have a somewhat disturbed sense of self, and it is called modesty. There is a scale on which one must fall with regard to sense of self, but the "right" placement is never clear (see pg. 32, Size of Person).

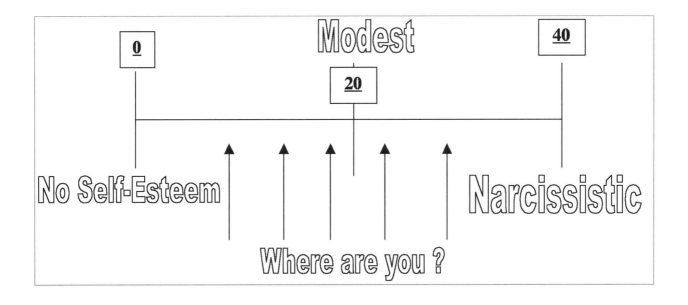

Illustration of kinesthetic learning.

Annoyance Checklist

Below is a list containing types of people and common events. If the situation or person described is annoying to you, place a check next to the statement. Then total the number of check marks.

_____ 1. A person telling me how to drive.

_____ 2. A person acting in an emotional manner.

_____ 3. Getting a telephone busy signal or put on call waiting.

_____ 4. A driver tailgating me.

_____ 5. To hear a loud talker.

_____ 6. To see an adult picking his or her nose.

_____ 7. A person telling me to do something when I am just about to do it.

_____ 8. A person continually criticizing something.

_____ 9. A person being sarcastic.

_____ 10. Receiving a telephone marketing call.

_____ 11. To know a person is staring at me.

_____ 12. To have my thoughts interrupted.

_____ 13. A person putting his hands on me unnecessarily.

_____ 14. A person constantly changing the TV channel.

_____ 15. A person giving me a weak handshake.

_____ 16. A person picking his teeth.

_____ 17. A person who "can't leave the party."

_____ 18. A person continually trying to be funny.

_____ 19. Being nagged.

_____ 20. To be evaluated critically by a stranger.

_____ 21. To have a person talk on a cell phone while they are with you.

_____ 22. To have to drive in heavy traffic.

_____ 23. To listen to politicians make promises.

_____ 24. To hear a person talking during a movie or concert.

_____ 25. To hear "loud" music played.

_____ 26. To be unable to find a parking place.

_____ 27. A person watching me work.

_____ 28. To hear a person swear.

_____ 29. To see overaffectionate demonstration between members of the same sex.

    _____   30. To hear disparaging remarks about a member of a minority group.

    _____   31. A man frequently referring to his girlfriends.

    _____   32. A woman frequently referring to her boyfriends.

    _____   33. Too much discussion of sex on a date.

    _____   34. To have to kiss an unattractive relative.

    _____   35. To see public lovemaking.

    _____   36. A person talking a great deal and not saying anything very important.

    _____   37. To listen to a sales pitch.

    _____   38. To have "too many" TV or radio commercials.

    _____   39. A person interrupting me when I am talking.

    _____   40. To see a person spit.

    _____   41. To have someone repeatedly urging me to take some food I do not want.

    _____   42. Not being able to find a noise in the car.

    _____   43. To discover that the library book is not there.

    _____   44. To see colors that clash.

    _____   45. To see an untidy room.

    _____   46. To find a hair in my food.

    _____   47. To have be around someone smoking.

    _____   48. The classmate who talks too much.

    _____   49. Not to be listened to.

    _____   50. To be given impractical suggestions.

               Total number of checks is _____

ANNOYANCES

The more things you check, the more things there are in the outside environment that affect how you feel. You are not in control of your emotional world, those annoyances checked are. One can get a fair assessment of his or her stress level based on how much annoys that person. One is much more easily annoyed on a Monday than a Friday because he or she has more control over his or her life going into a weekend than coming out of one into the work world. Not all the items on the list annoy everyone, and there is no one universal annoyance, so people do have control over what bothers them. Those items you checked don't have to annoy you; you have a choice. The items on the list may have more than just a simple reason for annoying us, a deeper, more symbolic meaning. For example, "someone criticizing my driving" is an almost universal annoyance. Why do people be-

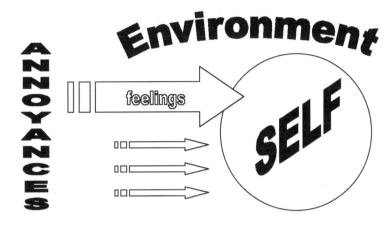

come so upset when someone criticizes their driving? Is it because they are such great drivers, with no room for improvement? Is it that most of us learned this motor skill from professional drivers, or did our parents teach us in this skill? Are our parents great drivers? Or is it the simple motor skills of driving have a greater meaning to us? Driving is a simple motor skill, and that is why while driving people can talk, dial numbers, eat, yell at children, look for CDs, and think so deeply that they don't even remember driving. When people criticize our other simple motor skills, we don't yell at them, "You take the wheel!" We don't threaten them or tell them to get away from us, "You don't like how I am driving? Well you can get out and walk." People generally show patience on the golf course if golfers are playing too slowly in front, but they may wish to run other drivers off the road if they are driving too slowly.

What could driving symbolically represent? At what age do people generally get their driver's license? At that age, how are we defined in the eyes of the world? We are 15 years old; we are not really children, not quite adults. Driving is the first time in a person's life that he or she has some sense of freedom, and "You" have the nerve to criticize how "I" control "My" freedom. Driving symbolically represents freedom (See pg. 17 and pg. 37, Garages and Birds). When the world was stressing the adolescent before he or she could drive, he or she could escape on his or her bicycle or scooter, but that would not get him or her very far. Suddenly the adolescent has some element of freedom. If others are trying to control and restrict that freedom, the response can be "I will destroy you." Unfortunately, in order to maintain this idea of freedom, we put ourselves in positions that may cause us to not only lose our freedom, but our lives, by driving drunk, too fast, or when we are too tired. People are more than the sum total of their motor skills; it is less stressful to admit you are out of control sometimes. What other annoyances on your list might have a greater symbolic meaning than the obvious answer: "It just bugs me." What items can you work eliminate from your list so that you can gain more control over your emotional world?

Now check your stress levels

Life Stress Scale

1. Death of child		100
2. Death of significant other		95
3. Divorce		85
4. Break up of long-term relationship		75
5. Detention in jail or other institution		65
6. Death of close family member		62
7. Major personal illness or injury		62
8. Marriage		55
9. Being fired at work		50
10. Military service away from family		45
11. Retirement from work		45
12. Pregnancy		45
13. Gaining new family member (birth or adoption)		42
14. Major change in financial state (for better or worse)		42
15. Major change in health or behavior of a family member		40
16. Sexual difficulties		40
17. Reconciliation with significant other		38
18. New boyfriend or girlfriend		38
19. Death of close friend		36
20. Change in job		36
21. Change in number of arguments with significant other (+ or −)		35
22. Taking on a mortgage		35
23. Foreclosure on mortgage or loan		32
24. Significant other change in job status		30
25. Change in responsibilities at work (promotion or demotion)		28
26. Son or daughter leaving home		28
27. Trouble with child's behavior in school or at home		26
28. Trouble with boss		26
29. Trouble with employee or coworker		24
30. In-law troubles		22
31. Outstanding personal achievement		22
32. Beginning or end of education		22
33. Major change in living arrangement (new home, remodeling)		20

34. Change in personal habits (dress, friends)	20
35. Major change in work hours or conditions	20
36. Change in residence	20
37. Trouble with roommate	19
38. Change to a new school	18
39. Major change in type or amount of recreation	18
40. Major change in social activities (clubs, dances, movies, etc.)	18
41. Taking on a second mortgage or loan less than $20,000	16
42. Major change in the number of family contacts	16
43. Major change in sleeping habits	15
44. Major change in eating habits	15
45. Vacation	14
46. Holidays	12
47. Receiving a ticket	12

Choose those events that apply to your life. Place a check in the box next to the events that have happened to you in the last 6 months or are likely to happen to you in the next 6 months. You may check events repeatedly that have happened more than once.

Total all the assigned points _____

Concept of Stress

Any time a creature is forced to adjust or adapt, it experiences stress. The only time a creature doesn't experience stress is when it is dead. Existence by definition is stressful. Any change people experience, whether it is perceived as "good" or "bad," is going to cause stress. The stress checklist has predominately negative events on it, but there are some events that are positive in nature, such as the items, "new boyfriend/girlfriend" or "great personal achievement." Since positive events cause the person to adjust or adapt, they are stressful as well.

The theory behind the stress checklist is that the greater one's stress score, the more potential there is for biological damage or illness. As stress scores increase, so does the likelihood of illness. An increase of approximately 100 points equals one more illness in the next 6 months unrelated to the bacteria or viruses present in the environment; this is due to the person's stress level. There are literally enough different bacteria and viruses in the environment so that a person could become ill with a different one every day of his or her life. As a person's stress level increases and is maintained at a heightened level, his or her immune system is depleted. The person's energy is directed toward coping with the stressors.

The person who is threatened engages the fight or flight mechanism. This mechanism allows the person to either attack the threat (stressor) or run away from the threat. A tremendous amount of energy is expended to engage this mechanism in order to deal with the threat; heart rate, respiration, and muscle tension are all increased. When another stressor is presented to the person, or an elevated level of stress becomes chronic, the depleted system collapses in illness. A very large percentage of the illnesses people experience are psychosomatically induced. The mind (psycho) put the body (soma) in a position to become ill. The checklist is designed to give the reader an indication of his or her stress levels and potential to develop illness.

There are specific events that are more likely to generate stress reactions than others. Those events that generate the greatest amount of stress have specific qualities. These qualities are unpredictability and uncontrollability. An event that has one or both of these qualities will, by definition, cause stress. Events that have both these qualities are the ultimate in stress producers. Examples of the ultimate stressors are: natural events, such as earthquakes, and manmade ones, such as war. The events at the top of the checklist are loss issues (see pg. 34, Hole in Trunk); loss of a family member, spouse, child, etc. When a person experiences a loss that is unexpected, it has both the qualities of unpredictability and uncontrollability; thus, it has the greatest stress potential and health impact.

In response to loss, people go through a grieving process. This grieving process has four stages. The first stage is shock and numbness. The loss has an unreal, incomprehensible quality. The next stage is the anger stage. The person becomes angry and attempts to find circumstances and people to blame and, ultimately, to punish. The next stage is the depression stage. The person blames himself and starts to wonder if he will be able to survive the loss. The final stage is the learning stage. During this stage, the person doesn't focus on the negative aspects of loss, as one does in the anger or depression stages, but on the positive features of the person and what he or she brought to the survivor's life.

The person who loses something as simple as his keys will pass through the stages. In the first stage, he is in disbelief that the keys are missing, continually checking the same places as if he had somehow overlooked them the first, second, and third time he checked. Then he enters the second stage, becoming frantic and angry, cursing. Someone may offer help and advice, such as "Where did you have them last?" The person looking for his keys then attacks that person, "If I knew where I had them last, I wouldn't be looking for them, you idiot!" The person proceeds into the third stage, worrying that he will never find the keys and is depressed that the keys must somehow be replaced. Finally, the person enters the forth stage, which is what he learned from experiencing the loss. He may get a spare set of keys in case he loses his keys again; this would be a positive response to loss.

When people experience the loss due to a relationship breakup, they often make decisions about future relationships in the anger or depression stage. When a person makes a decision in an angry or depressed state, that person's life will be focused on the pain of the loss, and her future relationships will be diminished in depth. The person in the anger or depression stage often will make statements such as, "I will never do that again. That was too painful." She has concluded that by not opening herself up to emotional hurt, she will be protected from future hurt. This is a false premise because, as she attempts to avoid the pain of the loss of intimacy, she has no intimacy in her life, so she is condemning herself to the cold, dull ache of loneliness. She has also taken the control of her future relationships out of her hands and heart and given it up to the person that hurt her due to the fact that the pain of the past relationship now keeps her from relating to future people in a meaningful way. The past is dictating the future. Since she is no longer in control of the depth of her future relationships, they will by definition be stressful. The person experiencing loss should realize that she must go through all the stages and forgo making any decisions until the final stage, the learning stage. Focusing on what were positive aspects of the relationship and doing more of those behaviors that are enriching to relationships, as is done at the start of a relationship, will make the future relationships less stressful. The beginnings of relationships are usually the consistently happiest times, and during this time, people tend to be giving more of themselves to the other person, rather than less of themselves as they do in the end. A consistently open and giving approach will assure the relationship a greater chance for success. A closed, limited emotional depth and protective approach will assure failure.

Parental Learning Style

Complete the following by reading the different statements. Then using an 8-point scale, distribute the 8 points across the statements. The statements can receive between 0 and 8 points, but total scores of all the statements on a line must be 8. Example: if *your* emotions can be told by: voice quality (0–8), general body tone (0–8), or facial expression (0–8) total across the row must equal 8. After each row is scored, then total the columns, giving you an Auditory score, a Visual score, and a Kinesthetic score.

A. My emotions can best be judged from:	____ my body tone.	____ my voice tone.	____ my facial expressions.
B. I keep current with the news by:	____ reading just headlines or briefly watching TV news.	____ listening to the radio or watching TV news.	____ reading all the newspaper when there is time.
C. If I have to communicate information to someone:	____ I prefer to talk, and often find myself holding things or tapping my foot.	____ I prefer to telephone since it saves time.	____ I prefer to write e-mails or letters.
D. When I am upset or angry, I usually:	____ can feel my body tense up.	____ tell others that I am angry and why.	____ say nothing and sometimes walk off.
E. When I am driving:	____ I shift in the seat and change the radio station often.	____ I turn on the radio or talk on the phone right away.	____ I like it still so I can concentrate.
F. When I am dressing, I think about:	____ what I will be doing and how comfortable I will be.	____ nothing, but I can always explain the choice I made.	____ the color and what I will look like in the outfit.
G. At a meeting or in a class:	____ I like it if there are breaks or chances to move.	____ I prefer if there is a discussion, so I can present my ideas.	____ I take notes and observe the other people.
H. In my free time, I usually:	____ do physical activities: sports, biking, gardening, etc.	____ listen to music, talk on the phone, go to concerts.	____ watch TV, go to the movies, or read a book.
I. When upset by a child's behavior I would discipline them:	____ holding the child's arm, picking them up, or spanking.	____ scolding, telling the child what he or she did wrong.	____ giving the child a stern look, refusing to talk to him or her.
J. When rewarding a child who has done something positive I:	____ give him or her a hug, pat on the back or a high five.	____ give him or her verbal praise, say what a "good job", etc.	____ smile, give stickers, put up the work for others to see.
Total	___ **Kinesthetic**	___ **Auditory**	___ **Visual**

Concept of Learning Styles

A learning style or channel is how information best gets into a person if it is to be retained for later recall. One's learning style is relatively fixed, and it is dictated by where a high score is. If it is in the Auditory area, the person would prefer to hear information; In the Visual area, the person would prefer to see the information; in the Kinesthetic area, the person would prefer to bodily experience the information. People are generally a combination of the types of styles and can receive and retain information from more than one channel. The following examples and comments about the different learning styles apply to some degree to those who scored significantly higher in that style and to a minor degree to those scoring slightly higher in that style.

VISUAL LEARNERS

Visual learners characteristically are unable to break away from a TV as they are so locked into that visual media and are concentrating on hearing the audio that they won't immediately acknowledge or even respond when called by name. There is no more primal memory than one's name, yet visual learners watching TV won't respond to that. They sometimes need physical contact to get their attention, to which they respond "Huh?" Visual learners don't like to go to movies because the other people talking interferes with their concentration. Do the visual learners tell the other people to "Be quiet?" No, that would be verbal behavior; they would rather give them dirty looks. The visual learner putting together a bicycle takes out the instructions, reads them thoroughly, makes sure visually all the parts are there, and lays them out in the proper order before attempting to put the bicycle together. When a visual learner meets someone and he says his name, moments later the visual learner is thinking "Who am I talking to?" because he is absorbing the new visual information and not the auditory information. Visual learners often have a strong artistic sense and are upset by clashing colors or patterns. They can end up in personal conflicts whenever people ask their opinion because they give an honest one, which might offend the person asking: "No it looks awful, oops sorry," demonstrating a lack of verbal impulse control. Since they often don't have good verbal skills, they end up in compromising positions. People may ask a visual learner to call them at a time, and when the appointed time passes, the auditory person is offended. The only excuse the visual learner has is "I forgot," which is not an acceptable reason. Often personal conflict is a matter of people attempting to communicate on different channels. If one has information that is important to him and he needs the other person to remember it, it is best to convey the information in the channel the other person learns in. In learning environments such as the classroom where the information is presented verbally, the visual learner can compensate by taking notes, but oftentimes that person neglects to reread the notes. When written material is presented in a class to the visual learner, it can often be overwhelming because he feels he must attempt to read and retain all the text material. The notes that the visual learner took can be an excellent guide for narrowing down the material in the text. Visual learners need to highlight the important text materials, making it visually jump out at them.

AUDITORY LEARNERS

Auditory learners need to hear the information in order for it to be retained. In a classroom, they are ideally suited for learning material presented in a lecture. However, oftentimes there are pressures to take notes, and this process interferes with the auditory information: "Huh? What did they say? I didn't hear, I was too busy writing." If a permanent record of the lecture is needed it is much better for the auditory learner to tape the lectures for later listening and focus his or her energy on listening to the lecture or discussion rather than note-taking. Auditory learners have great difficulty with reading textbooks specifically and any book in general. They have learned that sight (scanning the text) reading is a faster process than reading the material out loud, but it isn't for them. When they sight read, they retain very little of the information. Auditory learners will read a section and then wonder "What did I read?" They should be reading the material out loud, but if they do so in the presence of others, they will be criticized or labeled negatively: "Read to yourself, what is your problem?" Or "You move your lips when you read, what are you, stupid?" One can persist in engaging in a behavior that is labeled negatively or stop engaging in that behavior. To persist requires a strong sense of self (see pg. 19, Faces), and this is why relatively few auditory learners read for pleasure. Auditory people have trouble taking tests in a group setting because any noise is a distraction from the task of reading the questions. As the noise level increases, so does their anxiety level, which then makes it even more difficult to concentrate (see pg. 120 and 102, Brain Atlas and Stress scale). Auditory learners are the ones talking at the movies because they must verbally interpret everything that they see on the screen. Auditory learners often fail to pick up on non-verbal cues; they must be told they are being too noisy, and they often stand too close when they talk, making others uncomfortable. The auditory learner putting together a bicycle hands the instructions to someone else to read; then if things don't go right, he or she complains that the other person isn't reading it right.

KINESTHETIC LEARNERS

Kinesthetic or Bodily learners need to physically experience the material they are trying to learn. This is not possible in many environments. They are forced to try to learn information coming to them through the auditory or visual channels for which their physiology is not suited. In classrooms or offices, the kinesthetic learner is made to sit for long periods of time. The child or adult becomes restless and tends to move or wiggle around, eliciting comments such as "What is wrong with you? Why can't you sit still?" The person could be bored, and this is why he is twitching all over the place—because he is receiving information through the wrong channel. However, even when they are doing something they enjoy, such as watching a movie, they are wiggling. Kinesthetic learners are the ones kicking the chair in front of them in the theater, rocking in the seat. When they come out of the theater, they are exhausted from moving during every scene of the movie. If they don't like the movie, they are upset, thinking or saying "I had to sit through that; they ruined 90 minutes of my life." Brains are amazing things; they reason that the body must be involved in the learning process, so it moves the body around as information is coming at it. It is punctuating the information in terms of space and time (see illustration below). As the movie shows a certain scene, the body is in one position leaning back in the chair, and as the next scene is shown, the body is leaning forward.

What should the kinesthetic learner do in the classroom or office when information is coming at him through the wrong channel? Move and twitch around, but not engage in self-distracting behavior, such as continually sharpening his or her pencil or getting more coffee. When trying to read material, the kinesthetic learner is constantly interrupting the process. He or she will read a few pages, then get up to get a drink, return, read a page, call someone, return, search for a pencil, and finally decide he or she will read it before class. What should a kinesthetic learner do when reading? Read a little, get up and move around, and think about what he or she may have been reading, while avoiding engaging in self-distracting behaviors. The kinesthetic learner is going to take longer reading and maybe will only be able to get through a paragraph before he has to move around. The kinesthetic learner putting together a bicycle just starts putting it together without reading the instructions, and if he ends up with spare parts, "Oh well." Once a kinesthetic learner has done something physically, such as putting together the bicycle, he or she can do it repeatedly without much concentration; a construct of the bicycle resides in the brain/body of the

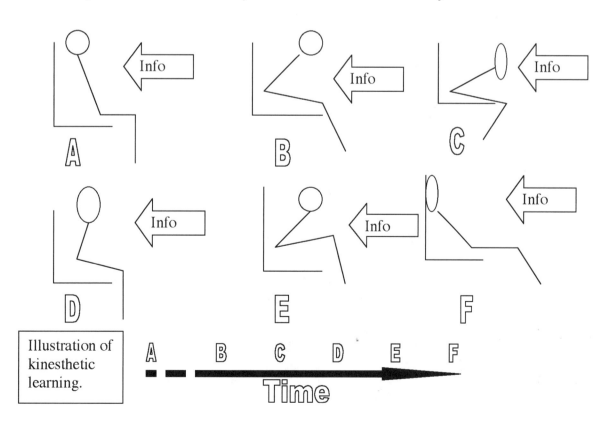

Illustration of kinesthetic learning.

kinesthetic learner. Kinesthetic learners often are athletes, having a very good body sense.

PARENTAL LEARNING STYLE

One might have obtained a different style on the *Discovering your learning style* than on the *Parental learning style*. This is due to the fact that the *Parental learning style* is testing for how communication is occurring in the role of a parent. In the role of a parent, people generally communicate verbally. For young children, learning most readily through the kinesthetic channel, this verbal style often does not match that of the child. Effective early childhood education programs utilize the kinesthetic channel for most learning experiences. Parents directing and disciplining children often will use the verbal channel exclusively to engage the child. When the child does not respond to the verbal directions, parents may resort to making comments such as: "Don't make me come over there"; "I'm going to count to three, one, two, two and 1/2, two and 3/4. . . ." The parent wishes he or she were better with fractions because he or she doesn't really want to get to three for he or she will have to get up, come over and engage in a kinesthetically/bodily response. That response may involve physically showing the child what to do (ideal for the child's learning) or spanking the child (not ideal learning for anyone). Often parents become frustrated with their children for not listening, but the problem may not be with the child. Rather, the problem is that the parent is providing the information to the child through the wrong channel.

This is an illustration titled *A House, a Tree, and a Person* by an 8-year-old. The nature of the parental interactions with a child can be symbolically represented in his or her continually evolving drawings. See main text pgs. 1–61.

Attention Deficit Disorder with or without Hyperactivity Checklist

Below are descriptions of behavior. Read the items and compare your behaviors, or the behaviors of the person whom you are evaluating, to that of friends and peers. Circle the number that most closely describes your behavior or that of the person you are evaluating. Total the scores for each section.

Attention

Rarely				Always
1	2	3	4	5
1	2	3	4	5
1	2	3	4	5
1	2	3	4	5
1	2	3	4	5
1	2	3	4	5

1. Works well without involving peers
2. Maintains working for reasonable amount of time
3. Completes work in timely manner
4. Little trouble listening for any length of time
5. Follows series of instructions
6. Is not distracted easily in classroom or office

Total score of items _____

Hyperactivity

Rarely				Always
1	2	3	4	5
1	2	3	4	5
1	2	3	4	5
1	2	3	4	5
1	2	3	4	5
1	2	3	4	5

1. Extremely active, must get out of seat often
2. Overreacts to sounds or movements
3. Excessive fidgeting, toe tapping, shifting in chair
4. Stands when chair available
5. Odd or limited sleep schedule
6. Constant movement throughout day

Total score of items_____

Impulsivity

Rarely				Always
1	2	3	4	5
1	2	3	4	5
1	2	3	4	5
1	2	3	4	5
1	2	3	4	5
1	2	3	4	5

1. Often acts before thinking
2. Frequently interrupts or talks over conversations
3. Frequently shifts from one activity to another
4. Difficulty waiting in line or for turn
5. Makes comments that one regrets
6. Constantly checking for messages

Total score of items _____

Social Skills

Rarely				Always
1	2	3	4	5
1	2	3	4	5
1	2	3	4	5
1	2	3	4	5
1	2	3	4	5
1	2	3	4	5

1. Avoids interrupting others' activities
2. Avoids being bossy or doing things that are bossy
3. Never teases other people
4. Always joins in group activities
5. Skillful at making new friends
6. Verbal and nonverbal communication clear

Total score of items _____

Concepts of Attention Deficit Disorder with or without Hyperactivity

If a person takes the ADHD checklist and obtains a score in the 15 and above range in any one area, he may have some of the characteristics of someone with ADD or ADHD. Of course, no single test can definitively diagnose anyone. A battery of tests is necessary to determine if someone has ADD or ADHD.

ATTENTION DEFICIT

People with attention deficit disorder (ADD) have difficulty focusing their attention on one specific task for any length of time. This inability to focus attention is due to the attempt on the part of the person to attend to everything that is going on in the environment. ADD is a physiologically-based disorder. The person with ADD has a lower level of functioning in the frontal lobe area of the brain (see pg. 120, Brain Atlas). The frontal lobes are responsible for directing attention toward the most important aspects of the environment for that individual. The area of the brain known as the limbic system is excessively active in people with ADD. The limbic system is made up of brain areas that collectively generate emotions and motivation (see pg. 120, Brain Atlas). People who have the combination of an excessively active limbic system and a less active frontal lobe control system end up with an over-responsive nervous system. An analogy is that the brakes (frontal lobes) of the car (limbic system) no longer work, and the car is running without means of control (stopping) unless it runs into something. So, the more distracting the environment, the more unfocused the person with ADD becomes. The person with ADD functions best in places with the least amount of distractions. Children with ADD function much better in individual learning environments rather than in group learning environments.

HYPERACTIVITY

Most people with ADD also have a hyperactive component. People with the hyperactive component of the disorder have a physiology that causes them to move constantly. People with hyperactivity have a great deal of difficulty sitting or staying in one place for any length of time. The hyperactive person's constant motion is often self-distracting as well as distracting to others. As with ADD, hyperactivity is due to atypical brain activity in the limbic system. The hyperactive person's body is in a constant state of fight or flight. Fight or flight is the mechanism that many biological creatures, including humans, use to deal with a threat. In the presence of a threat, the creature has two choices: to attack the threat (fight) or to run away to safety (flight). Because hyperactive people feel threatened, they are trying always to escape confinement.

All brains attempt to organize experiences and attribute meaning to them. Since hyperactive people feel threatened, they often attribute the threatened state they are experiencing to something external rather than internally-generated emotions. Hyperactive people often act in a counter-phobic manner: they attack what they fear. People act in a counter-phobic manner when they see a spider and step on it. "The best defense is a good offense," and the counter-phobic takes the offensive by striking first. Hyperactive people misperceive the normal behavior of others as potentially harmful and respond by attacking others in an unprovoked or excessive manner. This counter-phobic mode of relating to others is the root of many conflicts in hyperactive people's lives.

IMPULSIVENESS

A characteristic of people with attention deficit disorder with hyperactivity is that they are impulsive. They act without thinking through the consequences of their actions. Impulsivity is a product of the reduced frontal lobe activity, which, besides directing attention, controls reasoning abilities. ADHD people will see an object or generate a thought and then must immediately obtain the object or act on the thought. Impulsiveness can create much interpersonal conflict in ADHD peoples' lives (see pg. 24, Hands). Although frontal lobe activity is reduced, this does not reduce the intelligence capacity of people with ADD or ADHD; in fact, most have normal or above-average IQs.

SOCIAL PROBLEMS AND SELF-IMAGE

Social interactions take time to develop if they are going to have any depth to them. People with ADHD have trouble maintaining an interaction due to their distractibility, impulsivity, and their constant movement (see pg. 24, Hands). These characteristics affect ADHD people socially. For example, during a social interaction, the person with ADHD tends not to pay attention long enough to find out what the other person is saying or wanting, so the other person becomes frustrated; when the other person engages the person with ADHD, the ADHD person will often impulsively interrupt the other person or take what he wants from the other person without asking appropriately; finally, the person with ADHD will physically move in and out of interactions with other people to such an extent that the other people will be unsure that the ADHD person is even *involved* in an interaction at all. An example: a child comes up to the ADHD child and asks if he wants to play ball. The impulsive ADHD child will see the ball, hit it out of the other child's hands, kick it, and then chase after it. This is the ADHD child's way of saying "Yes," but none of it is socially appropriate. The other child will be left standing there, disliking the ADHD child. If the ADHD child has enough of these interactions, he may be collectively regarded as a "brat" or worse. These negative interactions and associated self-messages can build up and lead to a self-image that is similarly negative. People with ADHD often need a lot of opportunities to develop social skills and training on what is and isn't appropriate social interaction. These are best addressed in group socialization therapy.

ANXIOUS AND DEPRESSED CHILDREN

People with disorders other than ADD or ADHD may appear to have either ADD or ADHD. A person with an anxiety disorder can appear hyper-attentive and easily distracted just like a person with ADD. A person with an anxiety disorder will become unfocused and overly attentive in environments that are anxiety-provoking. Only environments that contain a potential threat to the person with an anxiety disorder will elicit the unfocused behavior. Generally speaking, the anxious person is anxious only in limited environments where the person is fearful something harmful is going to happen. For example, when a person who is afraid of spiders is somewhere he thinks there might be a lot of spiders, such as a basement, he is constantly looking for spiders or evidence of spiders. When the person with an anxiety disorder is removed from the threatening environment (basement), the unfocused behavior subsides. The ADD person, because of his physiological condition, is hyper-attentive in all environments.

A depressed person may appear similar in behavior to a person with ADHD who is in constant movement. Depressed people are attempting to distract themselves from their depressive thoughts by moving from one activity to another. If he continuously does something, he doesn't have time to focus on his concerns. The depressed person will even appear to be enjoying himself, but when he is slowed down and asked what it was he liked doing on that day, he will reply, "Nothing." The cause of the depressed person's hyperactivity is psychologically based; he is defending himself from negative thoughts by doing something compulsively. The person with hyperactivity, on the other hand, is in constant movement at all times because of his physiology, not due to an attempt to prevent thought.

It is critical to be very careful when diagnosing a disorder. The next step after diagnosing a disorder is coming up with a treatment. Prescribing the right treatment is only possible with the right diagnosis, and if that treatment involves medication, that medication will have side effects. It is crucial that the benefits of the medication are weighed against the side effects of that medication, and making a proper diagnosis allows for this to occur. This is especially true of treating children with medication. Also, just treating the physiology of the disorder doesn't cause the person to develop social skills and a new self-image. Therapy *as well as* medical treatment is necessary for those changes to occur.

This is an illustration titled *Dada* by a 6-year-old. Children act in impulsive ways, such as blurting out comments or creating unflattering representations of people. This is why it is critical to understand where a child is developmentally before becoming concerned about his or her level of functioning.

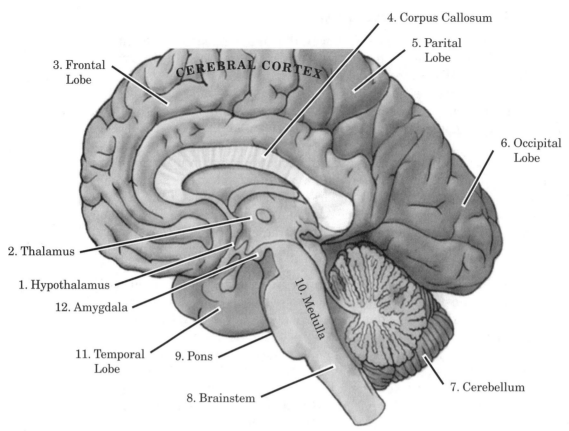

BRAIN ATLAS

1. **The Hypothalamus** controls motivation: The Sexual and Aggressive drive, along with thirst and hunger.
2. **The Thalamus** is the relay between lower brain structures and the cortex.
3. **The Frontal Lobe** controls thought processes and reasoning ability, maintaining control over the more primitive emotional and motivational centers, collectively called the *Limbic system*. *Limbic system* consists of structures 1, 2, 7, 8, 9, and 10.
4. **The Corpus Callosum** is a bundle of nerves that connects the two hemispheres of the cortex.
5. **The Parital Lobe** controls motor abilities and sensory experiences. Motor abilities involve precise movements and the sensation necessary to allow those movements, such as drawing.
6. **The Occipital Lobe** processes visual information.
7. **The Cerebellum** controls large motor movements, such as kicking a ball.
8. **The Structures of the Brainstem** control life support.
9. **The Pons** generates and regulates sleep.
10. **The Medulla** controls heart rate and respiration.
11. **The Temporal Lobe** processes auditory information and direction of aggressive responses; it is connected to the amygdala.
12. **The Amygdala** is involved in the production of aggressive responses.

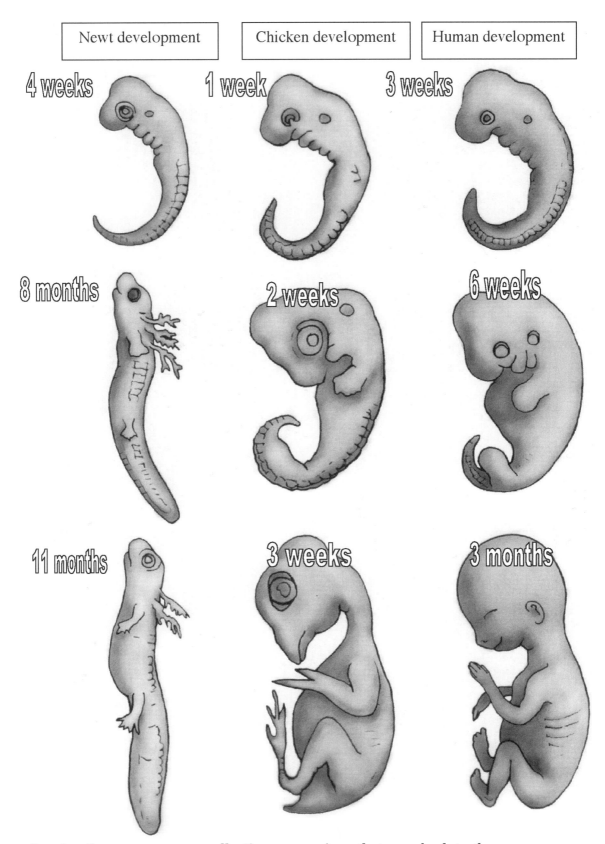

Newt development   Chicken development   Human development

4 weeks   1 week   3 weeks

8 months   2 weeks   6 weeks

11 months   3 weeks   3 months

Jungian theory proposes a collective unconscious that goes back to the beginnings of life on earth. The shared early biological heritage is evident in primal development of different species (See pg. 2, Introduction).

Here are examples of the identical brain structures found in different species, reflecting the biologically-shared heritage proposed by Jung and his contention that certain collective memories may be preexisting in all human brains (See pg. 2, Introduction).

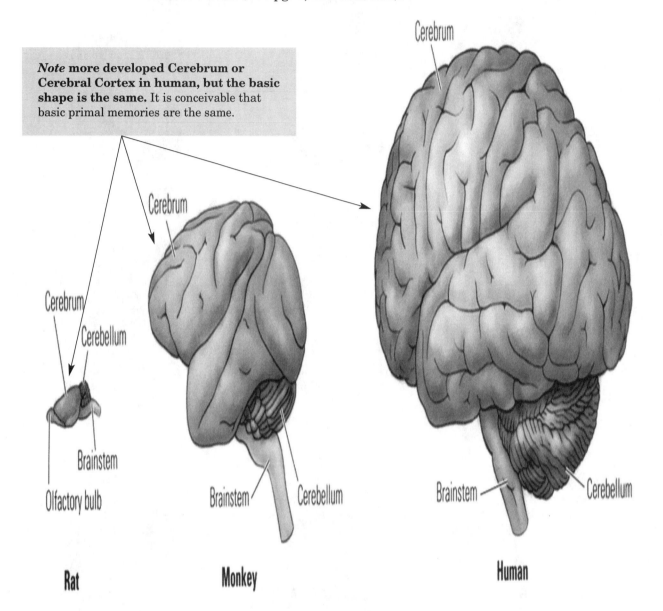

Note **more developed Cerebrum or Cerebral Cortex in human, but the basic shape is the same.** It is conceivable that basic primal memories are the same.

Cerebrum

Cerebrum

Cerebrum

Cerebellum

Brainstem

Olfactory bulb

Brainstem   Cerebellum

Brainstem   Cerebellum

Rat   **Monkey**   **Human**

Temperament Assessment Scale

Read the statements and assign a value. Chart on the next page. Once you have charted your-self, return to the scale *and fill it out for someone you know well to see how your temperaments match. Then chart the other person.*

1. *Activity level:* How much do you need to move around during the day? Can you sit through a class or meeting without wiggling or tapping your foot?

Active	You	1	2	3	4	5	Still
	Them	1	2	3	4	5	

2. *Regularity:* How regular are you in your eating, sleeping, and elimination habits?

Regular	You	1	2	3	4	5	Irregular
	Them	1	2	3	4	5	

3. *Adaptability:* How quickly do you adapt to a change in schedule or routine, a new place, or food?

Adapt quickly	You	1	2	3	4	5	Slow to adapt
	Them	1	2	3	4	5	

4. *Approach/Withdrawal:* Your reaction to the suggestion of being with new people, places, activities?

Approach	You	1	2	3	4	5	Withdrawal
	Them	1	2	3	4	5	

5. *Physical Sensitivity:* How aware are you of slight differences in noise level, temperature, or touch?

Not sensitive	You	1	2	3	4	5	Very sensitive
	Them	1	2	3	4	5	

6. *Intensity of Reaction:* How strong are your reactions to good/bad news, presents, winning/losing?

High intensity	You	1	2	3	4	5	Mild reaction
	Them	1	2	3	4	5	

7. *Distractibility:* Are you easily distracted?

Very distractible	You	1	2	3	4	5	Not distractible
	Them	1	2	3	4	5	

8. *Positive or Negative Mood:* How much of the time do you show pleasant, happy moods as compared with unpleasant or grouchy moods?

Positive mood	You	1	2	3	4	5	Negative mood
	Them	1	2	3	4	5	

9. *Persistence:* How long will you continue with a difficult task?

Low Frustration	You	1	2	3	4	5	High Frustration
	Them	1	2	3	4	5	

Temperament Assessment Chart

	Activity Level	Biological Habits	Adaptability	Withdrawal/ Approach	Physical Sensitivity	Intensity of Reaction	Distractibility	Positive Negative Mood	Persistence
5	Still/ Quiet	Irregularity	Slow to Adapt	Withdrawal	Very Sensitive	High Intensity	Not Distractible	Negative Mood	Low Frustration
4									
3									
2									
1	High Activity	Regularity	Adapts Quickly	Approaches	Not Sensitive	Mild Reaction	Very Distractible	Positive Mood	High Frustration

Chart yourself and connect the dots. Chart the other person and connect the dots.

Concept of Temperament

The concept of temperament is that people have genetically preprogrammed characteristics. For example, certain people tend to be more quiet and others more active, and this is their preferred way of being. This is not to say people who have a more active temperament can't be still; rather, it is just that that is not his or her preferred mode, and prolonged quiet would be difficult to maintain.

There is a range in which temperaments can be expressed. Often people who have different temperaments tend to be attracted to each other, "opposites attract." Actually, what is occurring is complementary people are attracted to each other; they see characteristics and skills in the other that they wished they had. It is difficult for two physically still people to become involved, just as it is difficult for two active people who are too busy to get together. In the beginning of a relationship, the people with opposite temperaments appreciate each other's different qualities. However, as both parties become more comfortable in the relationship, they tend to start to be critical about the very qualities that they were initially attracted to. The couple starts making comments such as: "Why do you always have to be doing something" coming from the still person and "Why do we always have to stay in?" coming from the active person. Rather than continuing to be accepting and unconditionally reinforcing of the people we care about, as we are in the beginning, we try to change them to be more like us (see pg. 43, Animal).

Looking at the temperaments of yourself and the other person you charted, those areas of greatest potential conflict or acceptance are where there is a large difference. Each type of temperament has its conflict potential.

ACTIVITY LEVEL

Certain people have greater activity levels, and some people operate at activity levels that come in conflict with most environments, specifically learning environments. People with high activity levels are diagnosed as having a Hyperactivity Disorder (see pg. 115, ADHD checklist, and pg. 24, Hands). Some people are more sedentary and prefer not to continually be doing something. A caution for this temperament is that a total lack of activity can lead to an unhealthy lifestyle.

REGULARITY

Some people need to eat and sleep on a regular schedule, and if they don't, their mood is adversely affected. People whose mood is affected by being irregular must maintain a stable pattern. If then don't, they are choosing to be in bad mood by depriving themselves of sleep and/or food, which for them maintains a stable mood. A significant percentage of the bad moods people have are due to lack of sleep. Research has shown that most adults are sleep deprived.

ADAPTABILITY

Some people have great difficulty adapting to change. They tend toward higher anxiety levels. It is commonly thought that happiness and sadness are opposite sides of the same coin, yet people can be simultaneously happy and sad, such as the feelings that events of great joy such as the birth of a child elicit. The truly mutually exclusive states are happiness and anxiety. One cannot be both anxious and happy at the same time. When people who have a temperament that is less adaptable can push to adaptability without overwhelming themselves, they increase their potential for happiness.

APPROACH/WITHDRAWAL

Some people are shyer than others, and forcing them to be more interactive will only create insecurity and anxiety. Providing opportunity for a person to interact and approach others at his or her own pace is better for overcoming shyness. Sometimes shyness is reinforced. The child withdraws, and others make a great effort to engage and draw them into an interaction, which is rewarding shy behavior with attention. A person with a more shy temperament will never become extroverted, but he can learn social skills that may lead to more opportunity for rewarding relationships.

PHYSICAL SENSITIVITY

Some people are more sensitive to the physical world. These people will not become outdoor types or become involved in contact sports. Forcing such children or adults into these activities will only lead to frustration and disappointment for all involved. We have two touch or pain systems; there is the light touch system and the deep pressure system. The deep pressure system overrides the light touch; one can reduce a light touch itch by applying deep pressure. Many people with ADHD are tactilely defensive, they are sensitive to light touch, and they experience it as painful or irritating (see pg. 115, ADHD checklist and explanation). In order to hold a pencil and control it, one has to have a light grip on it. The tactilely-defensive person puts greater pressure than is needed, which results in broken pencil lead and sloppy writing. Tactilely-defensive people prefer the deep pressure and seek out rough physical contact. The rough play and sloppy work may result in the tactilely-defensive person being regarded as a bully and a poor student.

INTENSITY OF REACTION

Some people have a great reaction to things and events, and others have controlled reactions. Some people's reaction to the slightest thing is "Whoo Hoo!" and other people's temperament is that they respond with a mild "Thanks." If a person who gets excited about everything presents something to the mild reaction type, and the response is merely, "Thank you." The high-reaction type will be disappointed in the response because it doesn't match his own. The high reaction type will respond to the lack of excitement with comments such as, "You don't like it, I will take it back." The mild reaction type will then try to convince the other person that she really does like the gift or suggestion. If people want to be accepting and unconditional in their relationships, they need to believe that the other person's response is valid and honest.

DISTRACTIBILITY

Some people are more easily distracted than others; their attention span is limited by their physiology. People with an extreme version of this temperament are diagnosed Attention Deficit (see pg. 115, ADHD checklist). Often classrooms present the distractible child with too much stimulation. Pictures all over the walls of the classroom may appear stimulating and rewarding, but for the distractible child, this environment is overwhelming. On the other end of the spectrum is the person who can focus his or her attention for long periods of time but sometimes may miss other salient or important information that is going on because he or she is so focused on what he or she is doing. This characteristic can cause interpersonal conflict when one party doesn't notice something the other person has done for him or her.

POSITIVE OR NEGATIVE MOOD

Some people see the cup as half empty and are physiologically incapable of viewing the cup differently (see pg. 15; Elaborate Houses). These are people who are candidates for medication to help mediate their imbalanced chemistry. Some people come from environments that don't expose them to anything but half empty cups. People from these environments are capable of seeing the cup as half full, but they must be helped to perceive it as such, and this often requires therapy. Similarly, the people who physiologically can't see the cup as anything but half empty must also be helped to perceive the cup differently even after their imbalanced chemistry is fixed. Just because medication helps improve that person's chemistry so that he can perceive the cup, it doesn't mean he will. All his previous thoughts have been negative, and positive alternatives need to be suggested. Medication alone rarely fixes moods; it should be used in conjunction with some form of therapy. Then there are some people who by their nature, regardless of environment, view the cup as half full, or even more positively: "Damn, I got a cup, now let's go fill it!"

PERSISTENCE

Some people have higher frustration levels than others, and they will maintain working on a task or developing a skill longer than others. There are also those who will give up easily, or try to get others to complete the task for them. Parents rarely are good educators in that they have expectations for what their child should be capable of doing, and if the child is in fact incapable or unwilling, this reflects negatively on the parent (see pg. 21, Eyes). Many times a task isn't completed due to the fact that it wasn't broken down into enough steps or pieces to ensure completion. A parent may demand that a child pick up the toys or clean his or her room and these

This is an illustration titled *Vampires* by a 3-year-old. In regard to the temperament of the child, the family often has to do the majority of the adapting, not the child.

tasks are overwhelming, so the child refuses or does a partial job. If the task is broken down into pieces, "Pick up the Barbies first, then the Legos," success is much more likely. Similarly, adults say they are going to get in shape today, or start eating right, or stop arguing, or stop smoking when any one of these is an overwhelming task and unlikely to be accomplished. If one makes the decision to eat one good meal or exercise one day, or cut back one cigarette per week, success is much more likely. However, there are some very persistent people who say they are going to run a marathon and start training constantly until they do.

More Drawings to Analyze

FIGURE 150

FIGURE 151

FIGURE 152

FIGURE 153

FIGURE 154

FIGURE 155

Bibliography

Buck, J. 1969. *Advances in the House-Tree-Person Technique*
Buck, J. and Warren, 1992. *House-Tree-Person Projective Drawing Technique*
Darwin, C. 1859. *The Origin of Species*
Freud, S. 1900. *The Interpretation of Dreams*
Freud, S. 1913. *Totem and Taboo*
Freud, S. 1895. *Studies on Hysteria*
Goodenough, F. 1926. *Measurement of Intelligence by Drawing*
Jung, C. 1964. *Man and His Symbols*
Rorschach, H. 1921. *Psychodiagnostik*

Illustration Credits

Pg. 4 Christian stained glass, ice crystal, and spider web from Kendall/Hunt photo library.
Pg. 4 Tibetan Buddhist Mandalas and Navajo sand art from Joseph Preston, 1998. *The History of the Mandala.*
Pg. 90, 91, 92 from Kolb and Whishaw, 2001. In the *Introduction to Brain and Behavior,* Worth Publishing.
Fig. 1–5, 27, 51, 52, and 66–69 from recreations of drawings by clinical patients at Menninger San Francisco Bay Area's Child and Adolescent Program.
Fig. 6–26, 28–50, 53–65, and 70–155 from drawings by students of Diablo Valley College.
Pg. 85, 89, 97, and 103 from drawings by Julia Pitner.

About the Author

Paul Pitner has been teaching Psychology and Early Childhood Education courses at Diablo Valley College for 15 years. He worked for many years as a therapist at Menninger San Francisco Bay Area's Child and Adolescence Program, where he conducted children and adolescent group therapy sessions, individual counseling with parents, and training and supervising M.F.C.C. and Ph.D. candidate interns in child group therapy. After working at this program for 7 years, it closed due to denial of funding, so Paul moved the program to the Family Service Agency of San Mateo County, where he continued in the same capacity but accepted the added responsibility of consulting with the state-funded preschools and doing individual counseling and group counseling with adult clients. Paul also started a consultancy with the Bridge School, a school for children with Cerebral Palsy, founded by musician Neil Young, where he conducted groups focusing on the skills and emotional issues involved in matriculating into a "regular" classroom. The school's children were completely non-verbal and communicated with computerized talk systems.

In his work with clients and students, Paul has obtained a vast collection of drawings. The house, tree, and person drawings in his collection number over 1,000.

He lives in Oakland, California, with his wife and 8-year-old daughter.

This is an illustration titled *Living in California* by an 8-year-old.